Experimenting with Babies

"*Experimenting with Babies* is a wonderful book, giving parents a hands-on way to understand their baby's emerging mind. The experiments are easy, fun, and nicely annotated with the real science behind them. What a fabulous way for parents to get to know their new child!"

—Lise Eliot, PhD, associate professor of neuroscience at the Chicago Medical School of Rosalind Franklin University and author of *What's Going On in There? How the Brain and Mind Develop in the First Five Years of Life*

"With the marketplace urging parents to buy all manner of things to make their babies 'smart,' Gallagher's book offers parents a view based in science on how much babies really know and figure out on their own. Parents will have fun with this book and gain new respect and awe for their babies' amazing capabilities."

—Roberta Michnick Golinkoff, PhD, H. Rodney Sharp Professor at the University of Delaware and coauthor of *How Babies Talk*, *Einstein Never Used Flash Cards*, and *A Mandate for Playful Learning in Preschool*

W9-CBT-220

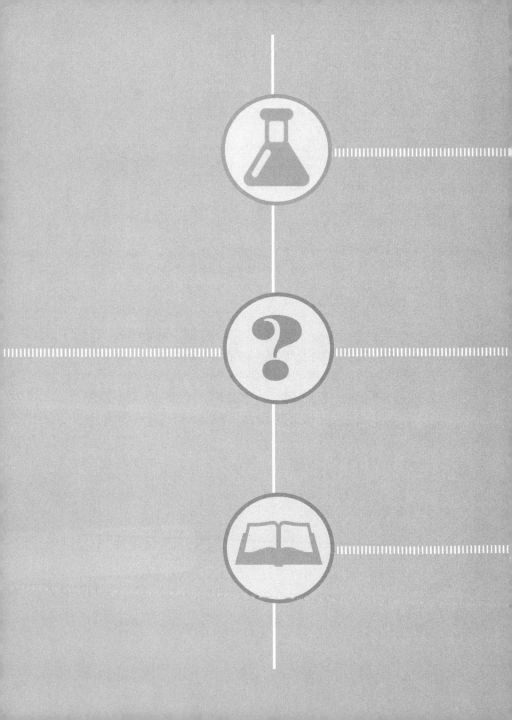

EXPERIMENTING WITH
BABIES

50 Amazing Science Projects
You Can Perform on Your Kid

SHAUN GALLAGHER

A TARCHERPERIGEE BOOK

tarcherperigee

An Imprint of Penguin Random House LLC
375 Hudson Street
New York, New York 10014

Most TarcherPerigee books are available at special quantity discounts for bulk purchase for sales promotions, premiums, fund-raising, and educational needs. Special books or book excerpts also can be created to fit specific needs. For details, write: SpecialMarkets@penguinrandomhouse.com.

Library of Congress Cataloging-in-Publication Data

Gallagher, Shaun, 1948–
Experimenting with babies : 50 amazing science projects you can perform on your kid / Shaun Gallagher.
pages   cm
Includes bibliographical references.
ISBN 978-0-399-16246-6 (pbk.)
1. Parent and child.   I. Title.
HQ755.8.G346   2013
306.874—dc23   2013021018

First edition: October 2013

PRINTED IN THE UNITED STATES OF AMERICA

19   18

Text design by Ellen Cipriano
Interior illustrations by Colin Hayes

A portion of the author's royalty earnings will be donated to Show Hope, a nonprofit organization that offers adoption grants to families and medical care to orphans around the world. Learn more at ShowHope.org.

To my children,
who are my favorite
science projects.

CONTENTS

Introduction

W hen I was a kid, I begged Santa Claus for a Radio Shack 50-in-1 Electronic Projects Kit. The kit consisted of a "circuit board" with numerous capacitors, resistors, LEDs, and a buzzer for auditory output. For each project, you would connect various components with wires and then flip a switch and see what happens. It was great fun, and it contributed to my continued interest in science and engineering.

Now that I'm a parent, though, I've outgrown the Radio Shack science kit and moved on to an experimental apparatus of significantly higher complexity: the baby.

My kids are the most fun, intriguing, surprising (and exhausting) research subjects I have ever had the privilege to conduct weird and wacky experiments on. I've spent hours upon hours trying to figure out the optimal way to hold a baby to get him to fall asleep quickly—only to discover, as many parents have, that what works for one baby does not work at all for another. I've tried at least 20 different techniques to get a toddler to eat his peas. (The winner: "Please, whatever you do, don't eat your peas.") I've tracked my baby's acquisition of fine motor skills based on how gently he touches my face—it progresses from painful scratching to awkward poking to soft whisker stroking. I've seen how early babies' unique personalities emerge. Even at a few weeks old, you can already sense how their gears are turning by the way they look at you and observe the world around them. And there is something especially fascinating about conducting research on babies, who are themselves conducting experiments all the time—which typically take the form, "What is this thing, and what does it feel like in my mouth?"

Before you begin experimenting on your own baby using the projects in this book, it's important to be aware of a few caveats:

- The projects in this book are not designed to assess your baby's physical or mental health, intelligence, or any other aspect of his motor, cognitive, or behavioral development, nor are they intended to tell you whether your baby is developmentally on schedule or whether he measures up. Rather, they're intended to demonstrate principles of infant development in a fun, easy-to-digest way. So don't approach these projects as challenges that your baby must complete in order to keep up with the Joneses' kid (or the Einsteins').

- Although suggested ages and age ranges are included in the projects, they should be considered fuzzy rather than firm, so don't worry if your child is not able to perform a certain task described in one of the experiments. When possible, I've included milestone information instead of a strict age range, such as "once your baby is walking independently."

■ In many of the original studies cited in this book, a number of children were tested but excluded from the results due to common problems such as fussiness, crying, or inability to complete a qualifying requirement. In some cases, certain results were excluded because a child's behavior was substantially different from the majority of those studied. So if you attempt an experiment, but your baby is not able to complete it or your results are quite different from those described in the study, don't worry! It's not out of the ordinary.

■ In adapting published, peer-reviewed academic studies to parent-friendly exercises that require no special equipment or training, I've had to take some liberties that may affect the degree to which your results line up with those of the source material. For instance, in most published studies, children are separated into groups, and each group is assigned a different condition. One group is the "test" group, and another is the "control" group, allowing the researchers to compare the results across the two groups. In many of the projects in this book, you'll instead conduct all of the conditions on the same child—your baby—separating each trial by a length of time. The former methodology is, of course, preferred in professional contexts, but because this is a book of at-home experiments, it's more practical for parents to simply repeat the experiments, rather than recruit a bunch of neighborhood babies for a well-controlled study. (If you happen to have identical twins on hand, you can more closely replicate the control and test model. Then again, you might not have that much free time.)

As you work through the 50 experiments in this book, I hope they give you new insight into the various fields of child development—but most important, I hope you come away with many new insights into your own amazing little science projects.

Soothing Scents

Age range: 0–1 month
Experiment complexity: Simple
Research area: Sensory development

 ## THE EXPERIMENT

Sometimes when your baby gets upset, nursing, which has a calming effect, isn't an option (such as when Dad's on baby duty while Mom takes a nap or a shower). If you have stored breast milk to use for a bottle, try placing a few drops on a cotton cloth. Then place the cloth a few inches from your baby's nose.

THE HYPOTHESIS

The scent of the breast milk, to which your baby has been naturally familiarized through nursing, will have a soothing effect on her. She will cry, grimace, and flail less than a baby who has been exposed to an unfamiliar scent or no scent at all.

THE RESEARCH

In a 2005 study, newborns were split into four groups. Babies in the first group had been naturally familiarized to the scent of their mother's breast milk. The second group of babies were familiarized to a vanilla scent through repeated exposure. The other two groups were not familiarized to any scent.

On the third day after birth, while getting blood drawn in a heel stick procedure, infants in the first two groups were exposed to the scents they had been familiarized toward (breast milk for the first group and vanilla for the second). Infants in the third group were also exposed to a vanilla scent—but for them, it was an unfamiliar smell. And infants in the fourth group were not exposed to any scent. The researchers found that the babies in the first two groups cried less and showed less distress after the heel stick procedure than the babies in the other two groups. They also found that babies in the milk condition exhibited fewer flailing movements.

It should be noted, however, that infant formula does not

appear to have the same effect as breast milk—at least not for breast-fed babies. In a 2009 study, newborns who were undergoing a routine heel stick procedure were exposed to the scent of their own mother's breast milk, another mother's breast milk, or formula. Only the infants exposed to the scent of their own mother's milk showed lower distress compared with a control group.

 **THE TAKEAWAY**

Using familiar scents to calm your baby is a great tool to have in your quiver of soothing techniques. But don't let that be your only go-to move. Other effective ways to soothe your baby include skin-to-skin contact, nursing, shushing sounds, rocking movements, and mellow music.

Baby Blueprints

Age range: 0–1 month
Experiment complexity: Simple
Research area: Cognitive development

 ## THE EXPERIMENT

Gather two pieces of cardboard or poster board, each about the size of a large postcard. On one, draw Figure A (on the left in the following illustration) and on the other, draw Figure B (on the right in the illustration).

While holding your awake, alert newborn, have a friend hold

the two pieces of cardboard side by side in front of your baby, about a foot and a half away from his face. Ask your friend to observe which of the two shapes your baby looks at longest, and which your baby looks at most frequently. End the experiment when your baby stops looking at the images. After a short pause, repeat the experiment, but with the positions of the figures reversed.

 ## THE HYPOTHESIS

Your baby will look longer and more frequently at Figure A.

 ## THE RESEARCH

It's well known that babies show a preference for faces not long after birth. But what is it about faces, exactly, that attracts babies? Do their brains have some sort of innate blueprint that describes human face structure in great detail, or are they attracted to more general structural properties that faces happen to have?

A 2002 study found that one characteristic of faces, top-heaviness of features (two eyebrows and two eyes above, but only one nose and mouth below), attracted infants even when presented in non-facelike illustrations. A 2008 study attempted to determine whether another characteristic—congruency of face shape to the inner features—might also attract babies' interest. Newborns between one and three days old were presented with the two shapes seen above, and a video recorder captured their eye movements. An analysis of the recording found that the babies looked longer and more frequently at Figure A, whose outer shape is congruent with the arrangement of the three inner elements, than at Figure B, whose outer shape is incongruent with the arrangement of the inner elements. The results of their study lend further weight to the hypothesis that more general structural characteristics, rather than a blueprint for faces specifically, could explain why babies are so drawn to faces.

THE TAKEAWAY

Could it be a mere twist of fate—or twist of face—that your gentle visage happens to have the properties that capture wee ones' attention? From a parent's perspective, that thought might be hard to countenance, but whether babies are drawn to faces specifically or just to their more general characteristics is a topic of interest only to developmental researchers. For you as a parent, the principal thing that matters is that your face delights your baby, so make sure to give her plenty of opportunities to see it.

Tools of the Trade

A high-tech pacifier has given researchers new insight into what grabs babies' attention. The pacifier uses a pressure sensor to measure the frequency and pressure of a baby's sucking. The sensor can be linked to a computer to generate auditory stimuli, such as speech sounds, each time the baby sucks. Babies as young as a couple of months old are able to learn that sucking the pacifier controls the sounds and will suck more forcefully to generate sounds they enjoy. Researchers have used these special pacifiers to determine whether a baby can tell the difference between two sounds. If a single sound Is played repeatedly and then a new sound is introduced, babies tend to suck with renewed vigor when the new sound is played. This "high-amplitude sucking" technique has been used in numerous experiments and has yielded significant data, especially about how babies learn to recognize and then acquire language.

You can perform low-tech versions of such experiments by observing changes in how frequently your baby sucks on a pacifier (or on a finger) as you present various stimuli, such as pictures in a book or sounds from a keyboard. You can also help your baby make cause-and-effect associations through other combinations of actions and stimuli, such as by safety-pinning a ribbon to her pant leg that will ring a bell or jingle a toy when she kicks. Over time, she will come to learn that her kicking controls the sound, and if the sound pleases her, she will kick more frequently.

3 # En Garde

Age range: 0–3 months
Experiment complexity: Simple
Research area: Primitive reflexes

 ## THE EXPERIMENT

Lay your relaxed, alert infant on her back. Gently turn her head to the side.

 ## THE HYPOTHESIS

If you turn her head to the left side, she will extend her left arm out and bend her right arm at the elbow while clenching her right fist. If you turn her head to the right side, she'll extend her right arm

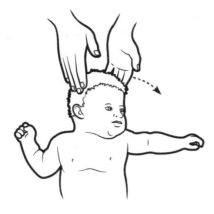

and bend the left arm at the elbow, clenching the left fist. Sometimes the baby's legs will also move reflexively.

 THE RESEARCH

This behavior is called the asymmetrical tonic neck reflex. *Asymmetrical* means the body responds differently on each side. *Tonic* refers to muscle tension—in this case, tension in the neck muscles. Though that's the clinical name, the reflex has been nicknamed the fencing reflex, because the baby looks as if she's assuming a fencing posture. The reflex was first studied in detail by German physiologist Rudolf Magnus, who studied posture and muscle tension in humans and other mammals in the early 20th century. The reflex is often present at birth or shortly after birth and disappears after several months.

While certain infant reflexes have an obvious purpose—such as the rooting reflex, in which the baby turns its head in response to stimuli near its mouth in an attempt to nurse—the asymmetrical tonic neck reflex is more mysterious. Some researchers have theorized that it is merely a strange byproduct of a developing nervous system, having no real purpose of its own. Others suggest that these reflexive movements somehow contribute to coordinated movements later in the infant's development.

 THE TAKEAWAY

The asymmetrical tonic neck reflex is the showstopper of primitive reflexes. It's the one you'll want to show off at parties while exclaiming, "*Science!*" Consider this the first among many strange behaviors your child will exhibit as she progresses from newborn to toddler (and beyond). Many of those behaviors will seem fleeting, as is this reflex, which typically disappears when your baby is around 3 months old. If your baby is a newborn, try running this experiment several times over the next several months and observe whether the reflex grows stronger or fades away and whether the arm movements become quicker or slower. You might not fully understand all of your baby's strange behaviors, but don't let that stop you from appreciating them. Some of the weirdest things your baby will do are also some of the most amazing.

Happy Feet

4

Age range: 0–3 months
Experiment complexity: SImple
Research area: Primitive reflexes

 THE EXPERIMENT

Hold your alert newborn upright, support-
ing her weight by holding her under the
armpits so that her feet are touching a firm,
flat surface, such as a hardwood floor. Then,
lean her upper body slightly forward.

THE HYPOTHESIS

Your baby will "walk" by moving her feet one after the other as you support her weight.

THE RESEARCH

The stepping reflex, also called the walking or dancing reflex, is one of several primitive reflexes present at birth. The reflex persists for a couple of months after birth and then fades away. Don't worry, though—it will reappear as a voluntary behavior later, usually between 9 and 16 months.

It was long assumed that the fading away of the stepping reflex a couple of months after birth is a result of brain maturation, but a 1984 study showed that it's actually the baby's strength-to-weight ratio that accounts for the gradual disappearance of the reflex. When your baby is a newborn, her legs will not have much fat on them, and so her muscles are strong enough to make her legs move when placed in an upright position. As the baby grows and her limbs become chubby, the increasing weight of her legs impedes the ability to make the stepping motion. But babies who had seemingly lost the stepping reflex exhibited it again when they were held waist-deep in water; the buoyancy of the water supported their weight, making leg movement easier. Researchers also noted that infants who had put on the most fat during their first weeks of life demonstrated fewer steps than infants who had less fat, which would support the hypothesis that the legs' strength-to-weight ratio may impede the reflex.

The fact that this stepping reflex is more continuous than once thought has implications not only for researchers who study motor development but also for those studying any type of dynamic system, in which multiple variables change at different rates over time. Indeed, partly on the basis of this experiment, researchers have suggested that a general dynamic systems theory could help shape our understanding of everything from embryological development to societal development.

 THE TAKEAWAY

Scientists hate hidden variables subtly creeping into their seemingly well-controlled experiments. In this case, the hidden variable was the baby's own physiology, so feel free to raise your nose in smug satisfaction that you've accounted for it and understand why the reflex disappears when it does. Repeating this experiment several times during the course of your infant's first couple of months will allow you to pinpoint when the stepping eventually stops—and it will also help prepare you for the stooped posture you'll soon assume more regularly as you help your baby learn to take voluntary steps.

This experiment also teaches a broader lesson: Your baby will occasionally experience setbacks in certain developmental areas, but take heart. Sometimes an apparent regression is not a regression at all, but a side effect of growth in other areas.

5 A Penchant for Patterns

Age range: 0–3 months
Experiment complexity: Moderate
Research area: Cognitive development

THE EXPERIMENT

Show your newborn baby some high-contrast patterns, such as black-and-white images of concentric circles, checkerboard patterns, or a simple drawing of a human face. Then show her some solid-colored images, such as red, yellow, or white construction paper. Make note of how long she gazes at each.

 **THE HYPOTHESIS**

No matter how young your baby is, even less than 24 hours old, she will gaze longer at the patterned images than the solid-colored images, and longest at the drawing of the face.

 **THE RESEARCH**

In 1963, Robert L. Fantz, a developmental psychologist studying observation patterns in babies, conducted an experiment in which newborn babies, ranging in age from 10 hours old to 5 days old, were shown patterned and solid-color images. He collected data on each baby's length of gaze at each image—considered to be an indicator of the baby's interest. The babies were found to gaze longest at the picture of the face, and longer at the high-contrast patterns than at solid colors. In fact, of the three babies younger than 24 hours old, all showed a preference for patterned images, and the youngest— tested just 10 hours after birth—looked longest at the face in three out of eight trials; no other image kept the baby's attention as much.

Fantz's experiment provides strong evidence that the ability to perceive forms in general, and the human form specifically, is innate and that from a very early age, babies' visual responsiveness to images varies according to the image's complexity. The results challenged the view, prevalent at the time, that pattern recognition and differentiation don't appear until weeks or months after birth.

 **THE TAKEAWAY**

Congratulations! You've just given your baby the infant equivalent of a Rorschach test. The results shouldn't surprise you. Your face is uniquely interesting to a baby, no matter her age. So make sure to give her plenty of face-to-face time. Also, because complex, high-contrast patterns tend to hold your baby's interest longer than simple, low-contrast patterns, give preference to the former when you make decisions about how to decorate a nursery or when you purchase toys or books for your little one.

Feet Lead the Way

Age range: 0–6 months
Experiment complexity: Moderate
Research area: Motor skills

THE EXPERIMENT

Introduce a jingly toy to your baby by showing it to her and shaking it. Put the toy in her hand and allow her to grasp it. Then touch her feet with the toy. Next, place the toy near your baby so that she can grasp it if she reaches out to it. Then place the toy near your baby so that she can touch the toy with her feet if she moves them.

THE HYPOTHESIS

Your baby will be able to touch the toy with her feet about a month earlier than she can reach out and grasp it with her hands.

THE RESEARCH

It's long been thought that babies gain control over their bodies in a top-down progression. First, they learn how to control their head movements; then their arm movements; then, toward their first birthday, they learn to control their legs and feet in order to sit, crawl, and walk. But experiments like this one suggest that babies can control their legs earlier in the process than previously understood.

In a 2004 study, researchers placed infants in a seat that allowed their arms and legs to move freely. During some sessions, they placed the jingly toy at the infants' shoulder height and within arm's length, toward the middle of their bodies, so that merely raising their arms would not make contact with the toy. During other sessions, they placed the toy at the infants' hip height and within leg's reach, also toward the middle of their bodies. On average, the infants were able to touch a toy with their feet at 11.7 weeks, about a month before they were able to reach for and grasp a toy with their hands (at 15.7 weeks). The researchers noted that by the time the infants were able to touch the toys with their hands, they still spent an equivalent amount of time touching the toys with their feet, even though the hands have the ability to grasp the toy and the feet do not.

The researchers postulate that babies are able to reach for a toy with their feet before they can reach with their hands because of differences in the anatomical structure of the hip and shoulder joints. The hips have a limited range of movement compared with the shoulder, which might mean the degree of control required for intentional leg movements is less than for intentional arm movements. Because the arms have a greater degree of movement than the legs, this might also mean that not only are arm movements more difficult to control but also it is less likely that a specific pattern of motion will already be familiar to the child. As with adults, practicing a particular pattern of motion—for instance, a dance step—makes it easier to perform, and so the practice that babies get making a low number of distinct leg movements (relative to arm movements) may give their legs an edge.

 ## THE TAKEAWAY

Some people might be surprised by the results of this experiment, but any mom who has experienced the third trimester knows not to underestimate those tiny feet, which probably spent a good deal of time practicing kickboxing in her uterus. It's natural to assume, though, that a baby would use her hands to reach for an object because that's what older kids and grown-ups would do. But remember: Your baby's developing body has a set of processes that have their own logic, which are not always what we might expect. Fortunately, as in many other cases, she'll try to improvise.

Response Under Pressure

Age range: 0–6 months
Experiment complexity: Simple
Research area: Primitive reflexes

 THE EXPERIMENT

Lay your awake, alert infant on her back. With firm pressure, press down on the palms of both of her hands and hold for about a

second. Then, also with firm pressure, press down on the soles of both of her feet and hold for about a second.

 ## THE HYPOTHESIS

When you apply firm pressure to her palms, your baby will almost assuredly open her mouth. She is also very likely to turn her neck, and somewhat likely to draw her legs up closer to her body.

When you apply firm pressure to her feet, your baby is very likely to extend her arms outward.

 ## THE RESEARCH

The mouth-opening response to pressure applied to the palms is known as the Babkin reflex, named after Russian researcher P. S. Babkin, who studied the reflex in the mid-20th century. In a 2004 study, two pediatric neurologists sought to extend his findings by testing what additional reflex responses occur when pressure is applied to the palms and other parts of the body, such as the arms, feet, and thighs.

They examined 106 newborns, each between 24 and 72 hours old, and found that 100 percent of the infants exhibited the mouth-opening response when pressure was applied to their palm. Nearly 90 percent turned their necks in response to the pressure, and nearly 70 percent drew their legs in. When pressure was applied to

their feet, about 88 percent of the babies extended their arms outward in response. The researchers also found that infants show
these and other types of reflex responses when pressure is applied to
other parts of the body, such as the upper and lower arm, although
in some cases only a small fraction of the babies exhibited a particular response to a particular pressure point.

Even extremely premature babies typically exhibit the Babkin
reflex shortly after birth, so it's considered a fairly reliable indicator
of reflex response. The researchers in the 2004 study note that the
fact that multiple pressure points can cause a variety of reflex
responses is useful knowledge for medical providers who are trying
to assess a baby's neurological condition, because it gives them
alternate ways to investigate the baby's reflexes aside from the stan-
dard Babkin procedure.

 **THE TAKEAWAY**

For parents, the Babkin reflex has a very practical use. In cases
when a newborn is not feeding well, pressure can be applied to her
palms to get her to open her mouth and nurse or take a bottle. You
might feel as if you're treating your baby like a marionette, but
when the kid ain't eating, sometimes you've gotta do what you've
gotta do.

I'm Hip to That

Age range: 0–9 months
Experiment complexity: Simple
Research area: Primitive reflexes

 THE EXPERIMENT

Lay your baby on his stomach and stroke either the left or the right side of his back, near (but not on) the spine.

 THE HYPOTHESIS

If you stroke the left side of his back, his left hip will rotate; if you stroke the right side, his right hip will rotate.

THE RESEARCH

This primitive reflex, present at birth and fading away by about 9 months of age, is called the spinal Galant reflex, named after Johann Susmann Galant, who first described it in the early 20th century. For some people, it persists past this point and can even last into adulthood. In school-aged children who still exhibit the reflex, it has been linked with certain developmental problems, such as bedwetting and difficulty sitting still. However, movement therapy can help address some of those problems. For instance, in a 2000 study, school-aged children who had persistent infant reflexes were assigned movement exercises aimed at helping them bring the reflexes under voluntary control. After a year of the exercises, they showed a marked decrease in their reflex responses and an increase in several academic measures, such as reading and writing skills, versus children in control and placebo groups.

At first glance, the spinal Galant reflex may not seem to have much utility, but it actually serves an important purpose during labor and delivery: The motion of the hips in response to stimulation to the back is thought to help the baby move through the birth canal.

 THE TAKEAWAY

Sure, this sounds like a fun reflex to experiment with, but once your baby has arrived, you'll likely be thinking, "Why on earth would I want to make my baby wiggle *more?*"

Don't Try This at Home

Several of the projects in this book describe how to experiment with primitive reflexes in your baby. One infant reflex you should *not* try to elicit is the Moro reflex, which is also called the falling reflex.

This reflex, first described by pediatrician Ernst Moro more than 100 years ago, occurs when an infant feels as if he is falling. The baby throws his arms out until the falling sensation ends and then draws them back in again. Some developmental researchers have posited that there's a good evolutionary basis for the reflex: If a caregiver accidentally loses her grip on the baby and the baby begins to fall, it is easier to catch him with his arms extended, increasing the baby's chance of survival.

The Moro reflex is apparent from birth and usually subsides within three or four months.

Normally, the sensation of falling that causes the Moro reflex is quite upsetting for the baby and crying is common afterward; consequently, don't try this on your own baby. (Your doctor may test for the reflex during a newborn evaluation, but unless you're a doctor doing a clinical assessment, there's no reason to put your kid through the distress.)

This Little Piggy Was Named Babinski

Age range: 0–24 months
Experiment complexity: Simple
Research area: Primitive reflexes

THE EXPERIMENT

Stroke the bottom of your baby's foot, from her heel to the base of her toes.

THE HYPOTHESIS

Your baby's big toe will bend up and back, and the other toes will fan out.

 **THE RESEARCH**

In 1896, Joseph Babinski, a French neuroscientist, noticed that in healthy adults, stroking the sole of the foot makes the big toe curl downward—but in infants and in people with certain neurological conditions and spinal cord injuries, the big toe curls upward.

In infants, the Babinski sign, also called the plantar reflex, occurs because their nervous system is not fully developed. By around age 2, the Babinski sign is replaced by the reflex seen in healthy adults. If it does not go away or if it reappears later in life, it may indicate a neurological problem.

 **THE TAKEAWAY**

Think of the Babinski sign as a tickle with a purpose. It's a simple, noninvasive test that helps doctors assess the health of the nervous system. From a parent's perspective, it's a reminder that aside from the developmental changes that are easy to observe, such as physical growth, improved coordination, and the beginnings of language acquisition, there are other, more subtle changes taking place as your baby grows and develops.

A Memorable Smile

10

Age range: 2–4 months
Experiment complexity: Moderate
Research area: Emotional development

THE EXPERIMENT

Show your baby a photograph of an unfamiliar adult who is smiling and looking toward the camera. Let her gaze at the photo for about 20 seconds. Then show her two more photos. First, show her a new photo of the person with whom she was familiarized, but in this photo, the person should have a neutral (nonsmiling) expression. Next, show her a photo of a second unfamiliar person, also with a neutral expression. Take note of which picture she looks at more. A few days later, repeat the experiment using photos of two more unfamiliar adults—but this time, neither of the adults should be smiling in any of the photos.

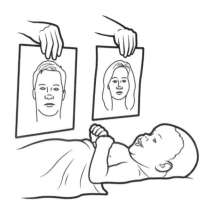

 TWEAK IT

If you have two babies of about the same age, you can test one with the smiling face and one with the neutral face, rather than testing both conditions on the same child. This more closely resembles the original experiment and reduces the chance that your baby's familiarity with the test procedure will skew the results the second time around.

 THE HYPOTHESIS

In the first part of the experiment, your baby will spend considerably more time looking at the unfamiliar face. But in the second part of the experiment, she may spend slightly more time looking at the familiar face.

 **THE RESEARCH**

A 2011 study involving 3-month-old infants found that babies who were familiarized with a photograph of a smiling subject looked significantly longer at the photo of the unfamiliar person than at the photo of the original subject, no matter the order in which they were shown. But with the babies who were familiarized to a subject with a neutral expression, they actually looked slightly longer at the photo of the familiar subject if it was shown to them first.

The researchers theorize that the babies who were familiarized to the smiling face were better able to recognize the face later, and because babies would be expected to prefer novelty over familiar things in a case like this, they weren't as interested in the familiar face—which would explain why they looked longer at the new face. The babies who were familiarized to the person with the neutral expression seemed to need a little extra time to recognize it later, based on their roughly equivalent looking times at the novel and familiar faces. The results of this study, the researchers say, cast into doubt the idea that facial recognition and emotional expression recognition are independent processes; rather, certain expressions appear to facilitate facial recognition. The results of this experiment are also consistent with similar experiments on adults.

# THE TAKEAWAY

Just look at that adorable little face. You almost can't help but smile at it. But if you still need prodding, now you have a firm scientific reason for doing so: It will help her learn to recognize you. One practical way to make use of this nugget of child-development knowledge is to create a photo flip book of family and close friends whom you want your baby to learn to recognize. Select pictures in which the subjects are giving big smiles. Their cheery expressions will heighten your baby's ability to recognize them later.

Out on a Limb

11

Age range: 2–4 months
Experiment complexity: Moderate
Research area: Motor skills

THE EXPERIMENT

Lay your baby in a crib. Loosely tie a length of soft ribbon to each of her wrists. Attach the other end of one piece of ribbon to a mobile or other toy above the crib, such that if your baby moves the corresponding arm, the mobile will move. Attach the other end of the other piece of ribbon to some other fixed point near the crib, making sure that this string, when tugged, will not cause any sort of motion or noise.

 THE HYPOTHESIS

Your baby will soon make the connection that her movements can activate the mobile. However, depending on her age, the specificity of her movements will vary. At 2 months old, she is likely to move all four limbs in an attempt to activate the mobile. By 3 months, she is likely to move her arms more than her legs. And by 4 months, she is likely to move the arm attached by ribbon to the mobile more than the other three limbs.

 THE RESEARCH

As far back as the 1930s, researchers have been devising and documenting studies in which babies learn to connect a spontaneous action with a corresponding outcome. In 2006, researchers set out to examine how this skill develops over time. In their study, which involved 2-, 3-, and 4-month-old infants, the babies first spent a little bit of time in a crib with strings attached to their wrists, but with the strings unattached to the mobile. This allowed the researchers to establish a baseline for the frequency of their arm and leg movements. Then, they attached one string to the mobile and gave the babies six minutes to realize that their arm movements caused the mobile to spin. Next, they detached the string and recorded the babies' limb movements for two minutes. As expected, the babies demonstrated more frequent limb movement than in the baseline period—they had learned that their movement caused the mobile to spin and were attempting (albeit fruitlessly) to make it spin again. With age, they became more specific about their movements. The 2-month-olds moved all four limbs at roughly the same frequency; the 3-month-olds moved their arms more than their legs; and the 4-month-olds moved the arm that had been attached to the mobile most of all.

The researchers then tried to test whether the infants were able to retain a memory of the causal connection even after an intervening period. Sure enough, they found that after a five-minute play break, babies in all three age groups continued to move their limbs at a rate higher than the baseline period.

The results of this study add to an area of motor-development research that attempts to explain how a baby with a large freedom of motion (that is, the ability to move various limbs in various directions) learns to constrain those motions to accomplish a given task.

 **THE TAKEAWAY**

Your baby is in the first stages of recognizing the connection between cause and effect. As she grows, she'll develop a more sophisticated understanding of causality. First, she'll learn that whacking things often generates noise or motion. Then, at some point, she'll discover gravity, and she'll delight in testing it by immediately dropping anything you hand her. It'll take her much longer to pick up on more complex instances of cause and effect, such as those involving delayed effects. She'll primarily learn these lessons through repetition, so have patience as she knocks her sippy cup on the floor for the umpteenth time.

Grasping Prep

Age range: 2–6 months
Experiment complexity: Moderate
Research area: Motor skills

THE EXPERIMENT

You'll perform this experiment multiple times, starting from when your baby is about 2 months old, and up until she begins to successfully reach for and grasp a toy. When she is awake and alert, but not fussy or crying, place her in a reclined seat but don't restrain her ability to move her arms. Sit facing her and talk to her to capture her attention as you introduce a small toy. The toy need not be unfamiliar to her, just as long as it captures her attention. Hold it in front of her, about an arm's length away. Spend about 30 seconds observing her arm and hand movements, paying attention to their speed and frequency as well as the distance and smoothness of the movements.

 ## THE HYPOTHESIS

Your baby will go through several phases in the weeks leading up to successfully reaching for and grasping a toy. In the early phase (8 to 10 weeks before successful grasping), the speed and length of arm movements will decrease. In the middle phase (4 to 6 weeks before successful grasping), the speed, number, and smoothness of arm movements will increase, and babies will move their hands closer to the toy than in the early phase. During the late phase (within 2 weeks of successful grasping), the speed, number, length, and smoothness of arm movements will be similar to that of the middle phase, but you'll notice fine-tuning of the direction of arm movement and an increasing preference for upward rather than downward movements.

THE RESEARCH

A 2006 study tracked babies weekly, starting when they were about 8 weeks old, and continuing until they were able to successfully grasp a toy (around 20 weeks, on average). Each week, the babies were either presented with a toy or tested under similar conditions but with no toy. This allowed the researchers to determine whether the babies' movements changed in the presence of a toy. Three-dimensional motion-capture technology was used to record the babies during the sessions, and the researchers' findings were based on an analysis of that data.

The analysis found that some differences between the toy and no-toy conditions were specific to a particular phase, but across all three phases, babies showed a continuous decrease in the distance between their hands and the toy.

The results of this study demonstrate that when babies are presented with a desirable object, such as a toy, they begin to alter their arm movements well in advance of being developmentally ready to actually reach for and grasp the object. By determining which aspects of arm and hand movement are specific to one phase and which are continuous, the researchers can construct further hypotheses about the developmental factors that produce these behaviors.

The researchers say the results of this study establish normative developmental behavior—that is, behavior typical of children who do not have developmental delays. The data can now be used to identify atypical movement patterns in children who are at risk of developmental delays, such as babies born preterm. For instance, they suggest that preemies should be expected to have a longer middle phase than babies born full-term, as a result of possibly impaired muscle tone and other factors.

 ## THE TAKEAWAY

Potentially months before your little one can actually grasp a toy that you hold out in front of her, she's already got her eyes on the prize, and her body is responding to the presence of the toy in various ways. By charting her progress toward the goal, you can see how different factors that affect her performance, such as muscle control and visual-spatial coordination, come into play. And now that you know that your 2-month-old really wants that toy you're dangling in front of her, even though she can't reach it, be kind and place it in her hands at the conclusion of the experiment.

Don't Try This at Home

In 1939, Mary Tudor, a speech-pathology graduate student at the University of Iowa, conducted an experiment on a group of orphan children in an attempt to determine what factors influence stuttering behavior. Half of the orphans she selected for the study stuttered and half did not. She divided the children into two groups, with each group containing both stuttering and nonstuttering children. Over a period of several months, she met with children in the first group, and whether they stuttered or not, she praised their speech and told them it was fine. Over the same period, she met with children in the second group, and whether they stuttered or not, she told them their speech was not normal and was in need of immediate correction.

At the end of the study—big surprise!—the children who were told their speech was not normal had become withdrawn and less likely to speak at all and their schoolwork suffered. The results of Tudor's dissertation were never published in any academic journal, but the study was brought to light in a 2001 article in the *San Jose Mercury News*, in which several of the study's subjects were interviewed. That article sparked a lawsuit that eventually ended in the state of Iowa agreeing to a substantial settlement close to $1 million- to be dispersed to several of the surviving orphans, who testified that they had sustained lifelong harm as a result of the "Monster Study."

Needless to say, experiments involving minors fall under greater scrutiny these days, and universities and other research institutions go to great lengths to ensure that children who participate in such experiments walk (or crawl) away from them just as happy and healthy as they came in.

13 Tongue Testing

Age range: 2–6 months
Experiment complexity: Simple
Research area: Social development and motor skills

 THE EXPERIMENT

Place your awake, alert baby in a car seat in a room free of distractions. Stand in front of her so that your face is about a foot and a half

away from hers. Look at her for 60 seconds with a neutral expression and don't respond to her attempts to communicate. Count how many times she sticks her tongue out and how many times she attempts to reach toward your face. Then repeat the experiment, but substitute a doll's face for your own and again count how many times she sticks her tongue out and how many times she attempts to reach toward the doll's face.

 ## THE HYPOTHESIS

Your baby will stick her tongue out most frequently at 2 months old and least frequently at 6 months old. For reaching, the trend will be the opposite: She will reach least frequently at 2 months old and most frequently at 6 months old.

 ## THE RESEARCH

A 2006 study involving 2-, 4-, and 6-month-olds sought to identify how a baby's oral exploration changes over time. The researchers found that when presented with a neutral-expression face, 2-month-olds stuck their tongues out an average of 4.6 times in 60 seconds, nearly double the average rate of 4-month-olds and almost 10 times the average rate of 6-month-olds. In contrast, none of the 2-month-olds reached, and the rate at which 6-month-olds reached was several times higher than the 4-month-olds' rate.

The study also found differences in behavior depending on whether the babies were looking at a human face or an object with human facial features (a mannequin). Babies in all age groups were more likely to stick their tongue out when looking at a human than a mannequin, and babies in all but the oldest group were more likely to reach when looking at a mannequin than a human.

So, at 2 months old, a baby's tongue serves a function that is similar to the function her hands serve in the coming months: It's a tool that allows her to explore interesting objects (in the case of the doll or mannequin) and react to unusual social situations (such as a face that gazes at her but doesn't initiate or respond to communication). By about 4 months, the hands are starting to take the place of the tongue, and by 6 months, she will rely much more heavily on reaching.

 **THE TAKEAWAY**

As adults, we don't think of our tongues as a particularly effective (or hygienic) way to get to know the world around us, but when you're an infant and haven't yet gained full control of your limbs, the simple act of sticking out your tongue is about all you've got, so you make do. Because the tongue is so important as a sensory tool to young babies, resist the urge—within reason, of course—to keep your baby from slobbering all over stuff. Hand her a soft, washable book or a plastic teething toy and let her go to town. She's not just salivating; she's learning.

Picture: Impossible

Age range: 3–6 months
Experiment complexity: Moderate
Research area: Cognitive development

 THE EXPERIMENT

Show your child a two-dimensional picture of a structurally possible three-dimensional object and a structurally impossible three-dimensional object (such as the pictures shown below).

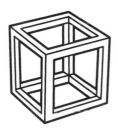 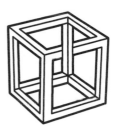

THE HYPOTHESIS

Your child will spend more time looking at the picture of the impossible object and will be more likely to explore the impossible picture with his hands by reaching, rubbing, or patting.

THE RESEARCH

A 2007 study involving 4-month-old babies gauged their interest in several two-dimensional pictures of 3D objects by tracking how long they looked at each. The infants were shown a photorealistic picture of a structurally possible wooden cube, and a photorealistic picture of a structurally impossible wooden cube that had been modified in Photoshop. The babies, on average, looked at the impossible picture more than twice as long as the possible one. Even when shown line drawings of the wooden cubes that were not photorealistic and did not have any color, shading, or texture, the babies looked longer at the impossible picture, suggesting that merely depicting the visible surfaces of an object, without other depth cues, is enough to help babies construct a 3D view of the object in their minds.

In a similar 2010 study, 9-month-old babies spent more time touching pictures of wooden cubes that were structurally impossible than pictures of structurally possible ones.

These studies suggest that at a very early age, children are able to demonstrate sophisticated spatial analysis. Specifically, they are able to view two-dimensional depictions of three-dimensional objects, comprehend the objects' three-dimensional structure, and most astounding, distinguish between the structurally possible and the structurally impossible. This is no easy task. To view a two-dimensional image and discern the implied three-dimensional structure of the object represented by the image one must be able to analyze visual cues such as linear perspective, texture, shadows, and junctions to infer depth.

 **THE TAKEAWAY**

You might think that at 4 months, your baby's spatial skills are still rudimentary—after all, he's only recently learned to reach for objects, and it'll be a few years before he can aim at the toilet with any accuracy. But this study reveals that there are some extremely complicated calculations going on in that cute little head. Don't underestimate him. Rather, help him further develop his spatial recognition skills by exposing him to artwork with various depth cues, and feel free to mix in works by the likes of M. C. Escher, who specialized in depicting scenes that would be structurally impossible in real life.

Pitch Patterns

Age range: 3–9 months
Experiment complexity: Moderate
Research area: Musical development

 THE EXPERIMENT

For this experiment, you'll need to classify the types of sounds your baby makes into two pitch profile categories, depending on whether they rise or fall in pitch. In a notebook, divide a page into two sections. Label one section "Trailing Rise." This will encompass sounds that have a simple rise in pitch, those that fall in pitch but then rise again, and those that make more than one shift in pitch direction but end with a rise in pitch. Label the other section "Trailing Fall." This will encompass sounds that have a simple fall in pitch, those that rise in pitch but then fall again, and those that make more than one shift in pitch direction but end with a fall in pitch.

During a period of unstructured play time (a minimum of 15 minutes, but up to an hour if you have the time), make note of any pleasurable "cooing" sounds your baby makes (exclude shrieks and squeals) and place a mark in the category that best fits its pitch profile.

You can repeat this experiment each month between 3 and 9 months.

 THE HYPOTHESIS

The trailing fall sounds will predominate. In fact, your baby is likely to make trailing rise sounds only if they are heard as part of your typical interaction with him.

 THE RESEARCH

In a 1990 study, researchers visited the homes of 3-month-old babies and recorded their vocalizations during hour-long free-play sessions. They repeated these sessions monthly until the babies were 9 months old. An analysis of the recordings found that more than 80 percent of the vocalizations were trailing fall sounds. A "rise-fall" pitch pattern was the most common pattern of all, constituting 30 percent of all vocalizations. When the researchers analyzed the recordings of the minority of infants who demonstrated frequent trailing rise sounds, they noticed that the babies' parents or caregivers also made trailing rise sounds and thus concluded that the babies were imitating these pitch patterns. The results of this study are in accord with earlier research finding that preschool-aged children also display a preference for descending pitch.

This was among the first studies to investigate the musical characteristics of the sounds made by babies of this age range. Previous studies on musical development had focused either on the vocalizations made by toddlers and older children or on babies' reaction to music that was played for them. Among the study's other findings: The pitch of the babies' voices did not differ by gender and did not become noticeably higher or lower during the 6 months that they were observed. One of the questions that the study raised was how, and to what degree, a parent's vocal patterns might influence the types of sounds their baby makes.

 THE TAKEAWAY

It'll be a while before your baby can sing "Somewhere over the Rainbow," but even at this tender age, he's hard at work, honing his musical chops by experimenting with pitch changes. And it may be the case, as suggested by this study, that your own expressions of musicality can influence your child's musical development, so let your own lilting melodies lead the way. Feel free to use this project as a jumping-off point to craft your own experiments. For instance, try to determine whether your baby responds differently when you use trailing fall sounds or trailing rise sounds or see whether your baby is able to imitate the sound profile you make.

Spider Sense

Age range: 4–5 months
Experiment complexity: Simple
Research area: Cognitive development

 ## THE EXPERIMENT

Show your baby each of the three images shown below. Image A shows a simple illustration of a spider. Image B shows the same image, but with some features reconfigured. Image C shows the same image,

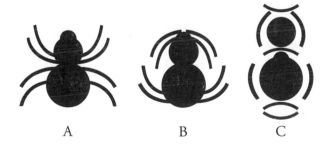

A   B   C

but with the features completely scrambled. You can present the images in any order you choose.

THE HYPOTHESIS

Your baby will look longer at Image A than at either of the other two images.

THE RESEARCH

Throughout history, spiders have been a common, and often avoidable, threat to humans. Being able to recognize a spider, identify it as a threat, and keep away from it is a skill that increases one's chance of survival.

In a 2007 study, babies were shown three images similar to the ones depicted above. The researchers found a statistically significant difference in the length of their gaze: They looked longer at the unaltered spider image (an average of 24 seconds) than either the partially reconfigured image (16 seconds) or the completely scrambled image (17 seconds).

The researchers posit that through a process of natural selection, humans have acquired an innate mental template of the general shape of a spider. They suggest that this template serves two purposes. First, it allows babies to rapidly acquire a fear response to spiders. Second, it allows humans throughout their life to rapidly detect the presence of a spider and avoid it. Such an inborn ability is not without precedent. The researchers point out that babies exhibit early fear responses to other dangers that small children have encountered throughout history, such as a fear of heights and a fear of adult males. The results of this experiment suggest that a similar survival instinct is at work when it comes to recognizing the shape of spiders.

 ## THE TAKEAWAY

Hey, cool! Your baby's got her own Spidey-sense! It may not turn her into a superhero, but it definitely demonstrates that she's on the alert against arachnid evildoers. If you'd like to extend this experiment, try showing her pictures of other potentially dangerous animals, such as snakes, rats, or narwhals, and gauge her response.

Put an Age to That Face

Age range: 4–7 months
Experiment complexity: Complex
Research area: Cognitive development

 THE EXPERIMENT

You'll need to enlist the support of two helpers: a child around age 9 or 10, and an adult of the same gender as the child. Have them practice reciting a nursery rhyme, such as "Humpty Dumpty," so that their speed, rhythm, and intonation are roughly the same, and then record the voices of each reciting it alone. Now, position both of your helpers side by side in front of your baby, so that he can see both of their faces clearly. Then play the recording of the child's recitation and have both helpers silently move their lips in sync with the words. Note how long your baby looks at each face during the recitation. Finally, repeat the experiment using the recording of the adult's recitation.

THE HYPOTHESIS

Your baby will look longer at the child's face during the child's recitation and longer at the adult's face during the adult's recitation.

THE RESEARCH

A 1998 study tested babies at both 4 months and 7 months. They were shown side-by-side video recordings of an adult and a child reciting a nursery rhyme, while audio from one of the subject's voices was played in synchronization. When the adult's voice was played, the babies looked longer at the adult, and when the child's voice was played, the babies looked longer at the child, demonstrating that the babies were able to match voices to subjects who varied by age. The experiment was modeled on an earlier study showing that babies can match voices to faces based on gender.

There were a few noticeable differences observed between the 4-month-old subjects and the 7-month-old subjects. Across several trials, the 7-month-old babies were adept at matching voices to faces from the start, whereas the 4-month-olds' ability to match voices to faces improved in the later trials. At 7 months, babies who were regularly exposed to children (such as those with siblings) were best able to match the faces and voices. At 4 months, the level of exposure to children did not make a significant difference.

An additional analysis of the experiment determined that, independent of matched or mismatched voices, the 7-month-old babies showed a strong preference for the child faces over the adult faces, while the 4-month-old babies showed a weak preference for the child faces. Those preferences are consistent with those demonstrated in earlier studies, such as one in which infants responded more positively toward child strangers than adult strangers.

 ## THE TAKEAWAY

Babies can sense that there's something different between adults and children, and there's something unique about the latter that is especially fascinating. Well—you knew that, didn't you? You can now trot out a scientific reason for encouraging older siblings and cousins to interact with your little one. And feel free to repeat this experiment multiple times. Not only will it allow you to track your baby's progress at face matching as he grows older but it may even teach him a nursery rhyme or two.

Tools of the Trade

One of the problems with using live actors in experiments is the possibility of subtle variances across trials. For instance, if the goal of a study is to determine how babies react to speech delivered in a positive tone versus speech delivered in a negative tone, and a live actor is used in each trial, it's possible that in one trial the actor's delivery might be slightly more dramatic or more subdued than in other trials.

Because those subtle variances have the potential to affect the results, researchers tend to prefer using video and audio recordings and computer simulations and animations, when possible. That way, they can be assured that the presentation one subject sees and hears is exactly the same as the presentation that all the other subjects experience.

Indeed, experiments in which babies watch a scene unfold on a computer screen have been growing in popularity, not only because of the consistency they provide across trials but also because they allow researchers to create scenes featuring moving objects that could previously be achieved only by using traditional animation, which was often prohibitively expensive.

The Face Matches the Feeling

Age range: 4–12 months
Experiment complexity: Moderate
Research area: Emotional development

 THE EXPERIMENT

You'll perform the following series of tests twice: once when your baby is around 4 months old, and again around your baby's first birthday. In all cases, make note of your baby's facial expressions during the tests. First, have a friend smile and tickle your baby's arms and belly for about 10 seconds. Then offer him a sour substance, such as diluted lemon juice, on a cotton swab. Then restrain your baby's arm for about 30 seconds (but cut the experiment short if your baby seems distressed).

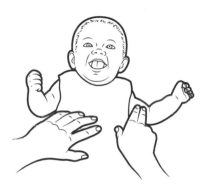

 THE HYPOTHESIS

Your baby's facial expressions are more likely to fit the situation at 12 months than they are at 4 months. Specifically, his facial expression is more likely to be joyful when being tickled, disgusted when tasting the sour substance, and angry when his arm is restrained.

 THE RESEARCH

Babies in a 2005 study were tickled, tasted a sour substance, and had their arm restrained at 4 months and again at 12 months. During each test, their facial expressions were observed and categorized. Researchers found that the babies at 12 months were more likely than they were at 4 months to demonstrate expressions befitting the situation, although even at 12 months, the predominant expression for all but the tickle condition was one categorized as mere interest. And in an additional masked-stranger condition, for which an expression of fear was deemed the appropriate response, only a small percentage of babies had unambiguously fearful expressions, and that percentage remained unchanged between 4 and 12 months. (The researchers hypothesize that facial expression alone may not be the best measure of a fearful response.)

According to a prevailing theory of emotional development, babies at birth have only two basic emotional states: a negative state, in which they cry or exhibit signs of distress, and a positive state. At this stage in their development, a wide range of negative stimuli will cause similar negative responses, and a wide range of positive stimuli will cause similar positive responses. But as babies develop, those emotional states become differentiated, so that one type of negative stimulus, such as a sour taste, will cause one type of emotional response, and another type, such as having an arm restrained, will cause a different response. This differentiation of emotions is called intrasituational specificity. There is a related term, called intersituational specificity, which means that emotional responses that are appropriate to a particular situation become less common in other circumstances. The 2005 study found that the infants they tested showed signs of increasing both intrasituational specificity and intersituational specificity. The findings offer some support to the idea that as infants develop, they respond to specific stimuli with increasingly particular facial expressions.

 **THE TAKEAWAY**

It's three in the morning, and your newborn is crying. Is it a hunger cry? A cry of pain? Is he wet? Is he scared of the dark? Is his swaddle too restricting? Does he want to be held? Sometimes it can be really tough to know what's bugging him. Parents often say that as they get to know their babies better, they become more attuned to their babies' cries and can distinguish an "I need milk" cry from an "I need a new diaper" cry. That may be true, but findings like this suggest that the job also becomes easier because infants' emotional expressions become more specific to the situation.

19 Stress Busting

Age range: ~6 months
Experiment complexity: Moderate
Research area: Emotional development

 THE EXPERIMENT

Place your baby in a car seat, and place the seat in front of a table so that he has a clear view of the table's surface. Sit about three feet away, so that he can see you if he turns his head. On the table, close to the car seat, place a toy that is highly stimulating to the senses, such as a fire truck with lights flashing and siren blaring, for about 30 seconds. Then, place the toy within your baby's reach for about a minute.

During this time, don't interact with him, unless he becomes distressed, in which case, end the experiment. Have a friend make note of your baby's general emotional state (positive or negative) and his behavior (such as looking away from the toy, sucking his fingers, or trying to touch the toy) throughout the course of the experiment. Later, repeat the experiment, but this time, interact with your baby in any way you wish.

 ## THE HYPOTHESIS

Babies whose emotional state becomes negative during the exercise will often employ coping techniques, such as looking at their parent, sucking on fingers, closing their eyes, hitting or banging the toy, or attempting to communicate verbally or nonverbally with their parent. In the first part of the experiment, in which you do not interact with your baby, coping techniques that include looking away from the toy or self-soothing are predicted to be the most effective in calming him, while withdrawal behaviors, such as trying to get away from the toy, are predicted to increase stress. In the second part of the experiment, in which you are permitted to interact with your baby, engaging with your baby by calling his name and trying to distract his attention away from the toy is predicted to be the most effective at calming him. In contrast, merely soothing your baby using gentle touches or vocalizations may actually increase your baby's stress.

 **THE RESEARCH**

In a 2004 study involving 6-month-old babies and their mothers, researchers recorded indicators of babies' emotional states and their behaviors in the first part of the experiment, during which their mothers were instructed not to interact. They then recorded the same information in the second part of the experiment, when the mothers could interact, as well as information about maternal responses. They found that many babies were able to self-regulate—that is, perform actions that prevented extreme distress—and that their mother's interaction also helped them regulate their distress levels. Among the most effective coping strategies in both sessions was looking away from the toy, and in the second session, when mothers assisted their babies to focus away from the toy by distracting them, it enhanced their child's ability to regulate distress levels.

Before the 2004 study, several other studies had examined babies' ability to regulate their behavior. For instance, a 1995 study of 5- and 10-month-old infants found that the effectiveness of certain self-regulating behaviors varied based on whether distress was decreasing or increasing. And a 1999 study found that maternal engagement helped toddlers regulate their distress levels. This most recent study added to that body of research by establishing that by 6 months, a significant number of infants were able to calm themselves in response to the toy, and when mothers were involved, that ability was enhanced. It also found that several specific infant and maternal behaviors were correlated with a rise or fall in distress levels, not only on their own but in combination with each other.

THE TAKEAWAY

Your baby is entering a transitional time in his emotional development. Until this point, he largely depended on you to comfort him and talk him down when he became upset. Now, he's starting to acquire the ability to deal with distressing situations on his own. On the one hand, you may feel proud that he's growing more independent. On the other hand, you may feel freaked out. There will be plenty of occasions when you'll have to back off and let him work things out for himself—but right now? So soon? Ah, not to worry. Clearly, in this transitional stage, a little help from Mom or Dad still makes a difference, so feel free to step in and distract him. Fewer tears are better for everyone involved.

Don't Try This at Home

Most experiments on babies are conducted according to strict ethical standards, but that hasn't always been the case.

In 1920, behavioral researchers John B. Watson and Rosalie Rayner conducted experiments on a 9-month-old baby dubbed Little Albert, in which they attempted to condition the boy to fear an animal by making a loud, scary sound whenever the animal was presented.

At the beginning of the experiments, the boy demonstrated no innate fear of a white rat, but he did become upset whenever the researchers made a loud clanging sound behind his back by striking a steel bar with a hammer.

During several sessions with the boy, the researchers made the clanging sound whenever he touched the rat, and soon the boy became fearful of the rat even when the scary sound was discontinued.

According to the researchers, a month after the initial conditioning took place, Little Albert still demonstrated fear when he saw the rat as well as other similar-looking creatures and objects.

Soon after, before his fear could be deconditioned, the boy's mother withdrew him from the experiments, and nothing is known about how long his fear persisted.

20 Propulsive Perceptions

Age range: 5–8 months
Experiment complexity: Complex
Research area: Perception

THE EXPERIMENT

Conduct this experiment twice: once around 5 or 6 months, before your baby has started crawling, and once around 8 months, after she has started crawling. You'll need to show your baby two similar toys, one of which has the appearance of being self-propelled (being able to start and stop motion on its own). One

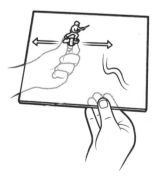

way to give a toy this appearance is to glue a small magnet to its base and place it on a poster board or other thin surface, then use another magnet underneath the surface to guide the toy around. Once you've gathered the toys (small plastic dollar-store figurines work well) and set up the magnets, briefly familiarize your baby with the self-propelled toy by showing her how it begins at rest, moves along the surface, seemingly on its own, then stops at the other end. Then familiarize her with the non-self-propelled toy. Let her see the toy at rest, then let her see you grasp the toy and push it gently to the other end of the surface. After a couple of repetitions, take a short break, and then alternately show her the self-propelled toy at rest and the non-self-propelled toy at rest. Use a stopwatch to determine how long she looks at each.

 ## THE HYPOTHESIS

Whether your baby looks longer at the self-propelled toy or the non-self-propelled toy will vary, depending on whether she has begun crawling.

 ## THE RESEARCH

A 2006 experiment involving 7-month-old infants found that they were able to discriminate between objects that were seemingly self-propelled and those that were set in motion by an outside force.

After being shown the toys in motion, the babies looked significantly longer at the toy that appeared to be self-propelled. A series of similar experiments were conducted in 2008 to test the hypothesis that the onset of crawling affects an infant's ability to discriminate between objects that are self-propelled and those that are not. In these experiments, looking times at the two objects differed between 5- and 6-month-old babies who had not yet begun to crawl and 8-month-old babies who had begun to crawl. In fact, looking times differed even among crawlers and noncrawlers who were the same age (7 months).

The ability to distinguish between objects that are and are not self-propelling is a valuable skill for a baby to acquire because it's a pretty reliable indicator of whether something is alive. This research shows that a baby's own ability to self-propel (by crawling) appears to be related to her ability to grasp the fundamental distinction between animate and inanimate objects. It also lends further support to the more general theory that a relationship exists between a baby's ability to perceive and process an action and her ability to perform that action herself.

 **THE TAKEAWAY**

Your baby's first successful attempts at unassisted forward motion do more than signal that it's time to secure the baby gates and move your valuables to higher ground. They also produce changes in the mind itself, creating a sort of feedback loop of developmental changes, with the mind and body trying to keep pace with each other. So, let's review: Your baby is now mobile and she will crawl toward things she's interested in. Your baby can now tell the difference between animate and inanimate objects and is more interested in animate objects. Expect this to be a scary time for the family cat.

Body Stretches

Age range: 5–9 months
Experiment complexity: Simple
Research area: Cognitive development

 THE EXPERIMENT

Show your baby the two pictures on the next page, side by side. One picture shows a woman with normal body proportions. The other picture is a copy of the first, but the neck and torso have been stretched and the legs have been shortened. Make note of which picture your baby spends more time looking at.

THE HYPOTHESIS

At 5 months old, your baby will not show a preference for either picture. But at 9 months old, he will look longer at the normal picture than at the distorted one.

THE RESEARCH

Although babies seem to understand the structure of the face early in life, it takes longer for them to understand the structure of the body.

For instance, in a 2010 study, 5-month-olds and 9-month-olds were shown side-by-side pictures of a young woman. One of the photos was unaltered, and the other was digitally manipulated to change the proportions of the neck, torso, and legs. The 5-month-olds showed no preference (based on looking times) for either photo, but the 9-month-olds showed a preference, albeit a slight one, for the unaltered picture.

A 2004 study on babies' perception of human body structure used images of bodies with scrambled parts, such as arms extending from the head, and found that it wasn't until somewhere between 12 and 15 months that the babies began to pick up on the abnormality. However, the 2010 study's results suggest that by 9 months old, babies are able to recognize the normal proportions of the human body. The researchers suggest that one reason babies might learn body part proportions before they learn body part arrangements is because body parts can move around (for instance, you can put your hand above your head in a way that might look like the hand is extending outward from it), whereas body part proportions are less changeable.

 **THE TAKEAWAY**

It's no wonder your baby gets to know your face before he gets to know your body. He spends a lot of close-up face-to-face time with you and other caregivers, and not as much time looking at your body from afar. Still, before his first birthday, he'll have picked up on at least some information about body structure. You can help him get to know bodies better by pointing to your own body parts and labeling them, and showing him where on his body those parts are located ("This is my elbow, and this is your elbow"). Won't be long before he's able to act out "Head, Shoulders, Knees, and Toes."

A Cappella
Strikes a Chord

Age range: 5–11 months
Experiment complexity: Moderate
Research area: Musical development

THE EXPERIMENT

For this experiment, you'll need two recordings: One in which a child sings a song without any musical accompaniment and one in which a child sings a song with musical accompaniment.

During the experiment, you'll use a technique that is intended to measure how much an auditory stimulus, such as a sound or a song, interests a baby. It's called the head-turn preference procedure, and it works like this: Direct your baby to look at a picture or pattern in front of her. When she looks at the picture, you'll begin playing a recorded song on your computer, stereo, or other music device.

When she looks away from the picture, pause the song. When she looks back at the picture, resume the song.

Conduct about a dozen trials, alternating the no-accompaniment and with-accompaniment recordings. At the beginning of each trial, direct your baby to look at the picture in front of her, and begin playing the song. Then time how long she continues looking and end the trial (and stop the music) when she's looked away for two seconds or more.

 ## THE HYPOTHESIS

Once you add up the listening times for each of the two recordings and average them out, you'll find that your baby prefers the song with no musical accompaniment (based on listening time).

 ## THE RESEARCH

In a 2009 study, children in three age groups—5, 8, and 11 months—listened to two recordings. In the first, a 9-year-old girl sang a children's song a cappella. In the second, the same recording was supplemented with instrumental accompaniment. Across all age groups, the majority of babies (58 percent) listened longer to the a cappella version; 28 percent listened longer to the version with instrumental accompaniment; and 13 percent showed no preference.

The researchers offer several possible explanations for the babies' preference for vocal music without instrumental accompaniment. It may be that babies' interest in the human voice—which has been well-established in other studies—is so great that the instrumental sounds just get in the way. Alternatively, cognitive limitations at this stage of development may lead the babies to prefer simpler auditory stimuli over more complex stimuli. This explanation is supported by a 2006 study, which found that babies prefer a song played by a single instrument such as a piano to the same song played by an orchestra.

THE TAKEAWAY

The researchers caution music educators that even though babies appear to listen longer to unaccompanied music than to accompanied music, that does not mean that they will not benefit from exposure to a variety of types of music. They recommend tailoring your musical selections to your objectives. If you're trying to teach your baby a simple children's song, you might be better off without a backup band. But if you merely want to teach your child to *appreciate* music, then break out the classical, Motown, Latin, jazz, hip-hop, space disco—whatever you're into, except Ke$ha.

Natural Interference

Age range: 6–8 months
Experiment complexity: Moderate
Research area: Language development

 ## THE EXPERIMENT

In a quiet room with few distractions, face your baby and repeat the word *boo* in a slightly drawn-out, falling intonation until she looks away, or until about 15 seconds have elapsed. Do this several times, until she begins to lose interest. Then, switch to the word *goo*, in the same intonation, and note whether her looking time is longer.

A couple of days later, perform the same experiment again, but this time, as you are conducting the experiment, play a recording of nature sounds that is loud enough to be slightly distracting but not loud enough to affect your baby's ability to hear the words you say.

THE HYPOTHESIS

When the experiment is conducted in a quiet setting with no distracting sounds, your baby is likely to look at you longer when you say *goo*, indicating that she has recognized the switch to a new sound. But when the experiment is conducted in the presence of distracting sounds, she is not likely to notice the switch.

THE RESEARCH

Infants in a 2008 study were placed into one of three groups. The first group was designated the "quiet" group. They were familiarized with *boo* in a quiet setting, and the switch to the word *goo* was also made in a quiet setting. The second group was designated the "distraction" group. They were familiarized with *boo* while distracting nature sounds played, and the switch to the word *goo* was also made while the nature sounds played. The third group was the "distraction-quiet" group. They were familiarized with *boo* while the nature sounds were played, but the nature sounds were removed before the switch to *goo*.

The researchers found that the quiet group had significantly longer looking times when they heard *goo*, indicating that they were able to recognize that a switch had been made. But babies in the distraction and distraction-quiet groups did not demonstrate longer looking times, indicating that they did not recognize that a switch had been made.

It may seem obvious that the presence of a distracting sound would make it more difficult for a baby to focus on a speech sound, and indeed, previous research had shown that infants are particularly susceptible to the "cocktail party effect," in which a number of competing sounds make it more difficult to focus on and comprehend any specific sound.

Yet despite the seemingly obvious result, an important conclusion can be drawn from this research that had previously been untested: Even when the distracting sound is not speech and occupies different auditory frequencies than the spoken words, it disrupts the baby's ability to process the speech and recognize the difference between the syllables. Adults are able to use a variety of acoustical clues to filter out background sounds, but it appears that babies in the 6- to 8-month-old range have not yet acquired that ability.

 **THE TAKEAWAY**

Time for a little empathy exercise: Imagine you're in a foreign country where you don't know the language, and you're trying to pick up any little tidbit you can. Now imagine that as you're listening to one conversation, 20 other conversations are going on around you. Distracting, isn't it? That's what it's like for your little one in the presence of background noise, so when you're interacting with her, turn off the TV, turn off the radio, and make it as easy as possible for her to listen to you and only you.

The Gestation
of Gestures

Age range: 6–9 months
Experiment complexity: Simple
Research area: Motor skills and language development

THE EXPERIMENT

Place your baby on your lap and let him play with one or more rattles for several minutes each. Keep track of how many times he makes noises or babbling sounds that are coordinated with rhythmic movement (for instance, repeating a syllable each time he shakes a rattle). Then place him on the floor and spend some time reading books and playing with toys. Again, note the frequency of coordinated vocalizations and rhythmic movements.

 THE HYPOTHESIS

Your baby will often make sounds to accompany his rhythmic movements, particularly when playing with the rattles. Vocal-motor coordination will be highest among older babies in the 6- to 9-month
range, and there will be greater coordination with arm movements
than with leg movements. In addition, rhythmic sounds (such as a
repeated syllable) will be more likely to occur during rhythmic movement than without rhythmic movement.

 THE RESEARCH

It's well known that both adults and children coordinate gestures
with speech when they communicate. In 1999, two developmental
researchers proposed a model for how babies come to develop a coordinated gesture-speech system. They rejected the notion that gestures

and speech are two independent communication processes and argued instead that they are two parts of a unified system of communication, in which each is closely linked with, and able to influence, the other. In a 2005 study, researchers examined motor-speech coordination in its early stages, at around the time babies begin to babble, to test the theory of a closely coupled gesture-speech system. They observed babies at home with their parents during structured playtime, which included a few minutes playing with rattles, followed by time spent reading books and playing with toys. They found that in each of the four age groups tested (6, 7, 8, and 9 months) the rate of vocal-motor coordination was greater with arm and hand movements than with other body movements, and rattle play produced the most frequent vocal-motor coordination, which increased from 6 months to 8 months and then slightly decreased at 9 months. Consistent with their hypothesis that the gesture-speech system is closely coupled, the vast majority of coordinated bursts of speech and movement were either movement-initiated (such as when a baby bangs his arm, then begins to vocalize) or synchronous (in which movement and vocalization begin at the same time). And when a gesture was made with only a single arm, it was usually with the right arm, consistent with adult gesturing.

The researchers in the 2005 study concluded that the results of their experiments support the earlier claim of a closely coupled motor and speech system. Based on their results, they proposed the following development scenario:

Babies begin to make rhythmic movements long before they begin to babble. By the time that babbling begins, the rhythmic movements are well practiced enough to "train" vocal activity, by giving it a rhythm of its own. This encourages what developmental researchers call reduplicated babble—the production of repeated syllables. Once babies begin to produce reduplicated babble, the coordination of rhythmic speech and movement becomes more frequent, which further strengthens the motor-speech link. By the time the child reaches between 9 and 12 months old (about the time that babies say their first word), the coordinated gestures are made mostly with the arms, while coordinated leg movements tend to fade out.

 **THE TAKEAWAY**

So strongly linked are gestures and speech that it can seem that crippling one might cripple the other. In fact, you may have heard some frequent gesticulators remark that if you were to tie their hands behind their back, they wouldn't be able to talk. As you observe your baby making coordinated, rhythmic movements and sounds, you are witnessing the formation of that bond between vocal and motor systems. You can promote this type of activity by allowing your baby to play with rattles and other noise-making toys, which they can shake to produce rhythmic sounds. Oh, sure, you might need to pop a couple Motrin afterward—but at least you'll know you're furthering your baby's development.

25 # Sizing Things Up

Age range: 6–9 months
Experiment complexity: Simple
Research area: Motor skills

 ## THE EXPERIMENT

For this experiment, you'll need two balls: a small one that your baby can easily grasp and hold with one hand and a larger one that your baby will need two hands to hold. Hold the small ball in front of your baby and note whether she reaches for it with one hand or both hands. Then hold the larger ball in front of her and again note whether she reaches for it with one or both hands. In each case, after she grasps the ball, let her hold and play with it for about 30 seconds. Repeat the presentations until you can determine a reaching preference: Does your baby prefer to reach consistently with a single hand or with both hands? If you are able to establish a reaching

preference, you'll then move to the next part of the experiment, during which you will present your baby with only the object whose size does not match her reaching preference. For babies who prefer to reach with two hands, repeatedly present the small ball and see whether she'll switch to a one-handed reach. For babies who prefer to reach with one hand, repeatedly present the larger ball and see whether she'll switch to a two-handed reach. Repeat these presentations about 10 times.

 ## THE HYPOTHESIS

Despite repeated opportunities to grasp the small ball with one hand (or the larger ball with two hands), your baby will continue to use her preferred reaching style. The younger the baby, the more likely she will be to persist with her established reaching preference.

THE RESEARCH

A 2009 study presented 6-, 7-, 8-, and 9-month-old babies with small solid balls (about two inches in diameter) and larger solid balls (about five inches in diameter) to determine a reaching preference. The vast majority of the babies responded mainly with two-handed reaching. A few preferred one-handed reaching. And a small number showed no consistent preference, but instead varied their reaching style based on the size of the ball. Of those who showed a one-handed preference, the majority continued to reach with one hand when they were repeatedly presented with the larger ball, and of those who showed a two-handed preference, the majority continued to reach with two hands when they were repeatedly presented with the small ball.

The researchers found that unlike adults, who can immediately adapt their reaching style based on their prior experience holding an object, infants in the age groups tested in this study had a difficult time overcoming their innate reaching preference, even after repeated exposures to the object. This suggests that the process of determining a method of reaching for an object that is appropriate for the object's size is a protracted developmental process.

THE TAKEAWAY

Sometimes, you'll find yourself marveling at how quickly your baby is able to pick up a new task. Other times, it can take her months to master what may seem to you to be a relatively simple skill. You might not know why, but there's usually a good reason. Sometimes, other aspects of their development take precedence; other times, a skill requires the convergence of several different developmental milestones before your baby can make solid progress. Whatever the reason, be patient—and be prepared to celebrate when your baby finally reaches the top of the hill!

26 Mirror, Mirror

Age range: 6–9 months
Experiment complexity: Simple
Research area: Cognitive development

 ## THE EXPERIMENT

Place your baby on the floor or in a high chair in front of a large mirror. Allow her to spend time looking at the mirror, and carefully observe her behavior over a two-minute period, starting from when she first looks at the mirror. Is she interested in the image of herself? Does she point to, touch, or otherwise interact with the image? Is her mood happy and friendly, scared, shy, or irritated? Does she seem to recognize herself in the mirror? If she moves a body part, does she notice that the baby in the mirror also moves the same body part?

 TWEAK IT

Invite a friend with a baby of the opposite sex to also conduct this experiment, and compare the results.

 THE HYPOTHESIS

Even if your baby is as young as 6 months old, she will spend a significant amount of the two-minute period looking at the mirror. Older babies (around 8 or 9 months old) will be more likely to smile or laugh and to attempt to interact with the mirror by touching or licking it.

THE RESEARCH

In a 2007 study, researchers observed the behaviors of three groups of babies (6, 8, and 9 months old) who were given the opportunity to interact with a mirror. The infants in all three groups spent a considerable amount of time, ranging from 85 to 90 percent of the two-minute total, looking at the mirror. At 6 months, the babies were attentive but did not display many attempts at interaction. The older babies, on the other hand, showed signs of interaction. More than 40 percent of the 8-month-olds and more than half of the 9-month-olds displayed behaviors that the researchers described as happy or friendly, which included smiling or laughing, and attempts to touch, lick, or otherwise make contact with the mirror. One finding that surprised the researchers was that at 8 and 9 months, boys made about twice as many attempts at interactivity as girls did.

Previous studies involving infants and mirrors had demonstrated that as early as 3 months old, babies' behaviors changed when looking at their reflections in a mirror. For instance, a 1972 study found that babies smiled and cooed at the image and reached out to touch it. However, other studies have concluded that the ability to recognize that the image in a mirror is a reflection of oneself does not emerge until after the first year, between 14 and 22 months old. For instance, in that same 1972 study, a test was devised in which a smudge of makeup was placed on babies' noses. Around a year and a half old, babies reached for their own noses when they saw themselves in the mirror, an indication that they understood the reflection to be an image of themselves; younger babies, however, failed to show such a reaction.

The results of the 2007 study build on these results and demonstrate that by 6 to 9 months old, babies will interact with a mirror image in social ways, and they appear to show signs of recognizing that the movements of the baby in the mirror correspond to their own movements.

 **THE TAKEAWAY**

Watching babies interact with their mirror images can be a lot of fun—and can also lead to a lot of smudges. You can take it a step further by spending time looking in the mirror together with your baby. For instance, you might look at her, then look to her reflection in the mirror, and see whether she looks at you or your reflection.

Capturing the Cup

Age range: 6–9 months
Experiment complexity: Moderate
Research area: Cognitive development

 THE EXPERIMENT

For this experiment, you'll need a medium-size cardboard box with one side open, and a large coffee cup with a handle. Seat your baby in front of a table. Place the box on the table at your baby's eye level, with the open side of the box facing upward. Now, put the coffee cup inside the box and make sure that your baby cannot see what's inside. Next, allow her to watch a friend slowly reach into the box from above. The friend's grasp should be wide, as if he is intending to pick up the cup by its rim rather than by the handle. Then, move the box out of the way so that your baby can see that your

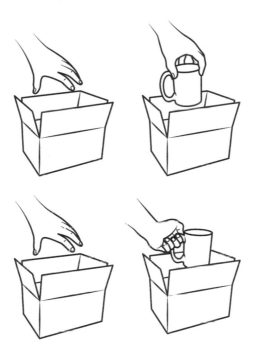

friend has indeed grasped the cup's rim, rather than the handle, and is holding the cup slightly above the table. Use a stopwatch to time how long your baby looks at the cup.

A few days later, repeat the experiment. Your friend's grasp should still be wide as he lowers his hand into the box, but this time, he should grasp the cup by its handle. Again, time how long your baby looks at the cup.

 **THE HYPOTHESIS**

Your baby will look at the cup longer the second time.

 **TWEAK IT**

If a friend has a baby of about the same age, you can present one of the two conditions (holding by rim and holding by handle) to each baby and compare the results.

 **THE RESEARCH**

In a 2009 study, 6- and 9-month-olds were shown a short video in which a hand reached into a box with either a wide or a narrow grasp. Then, they were shown two still images—one of the hand grasping the cup by the rim and one of the hand grasping the cup by the handle— and their looking times were recorded and analyzed. The analysis showed that the babies looked longer at the image in which the final grasp type (wide or narrow) did not match the anticipated grasp type. So, for instance, the babies who saw the hand begin with a wide grasp looked longer at the image in which the hand used a narrow grasp to hold the handle than the image in which the hand used a wide grasp to hold the cup by its rim. The researchers concluded that the babies were able to form expectations about the final grasp type based on the grasp type during the hand's approach, and they were surprised when the final grasp type didn't match, resulting in longer looking times.

The researchers concluded that babies as early as 6 months old are able to infer the size of an unseen target object based on the way a person reaches for it. This has implications for developmental researchers who study goal-oriented actions.

The researchers also noted that even though their study showed that 6-month-olds are able to infer the size of the target object based on the grasping style during the approach, an earlier study showed that infants don't themselves begin to adjust the width of their grasp according to the size of the object until about 9 months. Thus the results lend some support to the idea that babies are able to understand and make inferences about an action even before they are able to perform the action themselves.

 **THE TAKEAWAY**

You might think this little coffee cup exercise is no biggie, but all sorts of complicated processes are happening in your baby's head as she observes it. Not only does she have to size up the grasp style and connect it with the size of an object, but she also has to grasp the goal-oriented nature of the action. As your baby grows, she'll become even more adept at figuring out the goals of other people and anticipating their consequences. You can help her make those connections by pointing out the actions in a sequence and showing how one follows the other.

Tools of the Trade

A number of universities have baby labs devoted to conducting experiments on wee ones. For instance, Cornell operates the Behavioral Analysis of Beginning Years (B.A.B.Y.) Laboratory, which studies early communication, cognition, and language. Rutgers runs the Infancy Studies Laboratory, which is part of its Center for Molecular and Behavioral Neuroscience. Berkeley's Early Learning Lab studies how babies and young children pick up language and learn about probability and how to categorize things. Stanford's Center for Infant Studies focuses on vision and neurodevelopment, language, and social cognition. In the United Kingdom, Oxford's Babylab studies elements of language acquisition and visual processing. At Yale's Infant Cognition Center, researchers study how babies learn about their physical and social worlds. And UCLA's Baby Lab focuses on perceptual and cognitive development.

Most baby labs recruit their young subjects through a mixture of targeted advertisements in local newspapers and parenting publications and direct solicitation based on a review of recent birth announcements and public records. Babies who participate in a research study are often given a small gift, such as a college T-shirt or a "young scientist" certificate.

28 Grabby Hands

Age range: 6–10 months
Experiment complexity: Simple
Research area: Motor skills

 ## THE EXPERIMENT

You can conduct this experiment three times, when your baby is 6 months, 8 months, and 10 months old. Tie a toy to the end of a two-foot-long piece of string or attach it to the end of a rod of similar length. Place your baby into a seat and slowly spin the toy in a clockwise circular pattern at about the height of his nose. As he reaches for the toy, take note of whether he uses his left hand, his right hand, or both. If he successfully grasps the toy, let him play with it for a few seconds, and then repeat the experiment, but this time, spin the toy in a counterclockwise direction. You can repeat the experiment multiple times, alternating clockwise and counterclockwise spins.

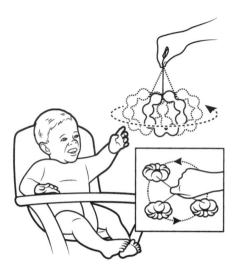

THE HYPOTHESIS

At 6 months and 10 months, your baby will not show a significant handedness preference, but will likely reach for the toy with his left hand when the toy is moving from left to right and with his right hand when the toy is moving from right to left. At 8 months, however, your baby will likely reach with his right hand no matter which way the toy is traveling.

THE RESEARCH

Previous studies had established that infants much younger than those in the test range are able to make predictive reaching motions—that is, they reach out for a moving object in anticipation of its arrival in a certain location, rather than reaching for it in its current location. A 2009 study sought to investigate the methods that babies of different ages use to reach for moving objects. Three age groups were tested: 6-, 8-, and 10-month-olds. A toy suspended by a rod was rotated in front of the babies, and the experimenters tracked the infants' reaching and grasping movements. When the toy rotated from right to left, babies in all three ages reached with their right hand more than half of the time; the 8-month-olds showed the strongest preference for their right hand, using it about 80 percent of the time. When the toy rotated from left to right, babies in the 6- and 10-month groups reached for the toy with their left hand more than twice as often as with their right hand. But the 8-month-olds reached for the toy with their right hand about twice as often as with their left hand.

The researchers knew that reaching for and grasping a moving object is a challenging task at all three ages, but less so for the older babies, and that handedness emerges over this developmental period. A previous study had also established that handedness is more likely to show up on difficult tasks than easy tasks. The researchers argue that the results of this study, in which the 8-month-olds showed a different hand-reaching preference compared to the other two groups, can be explained by the fact that at 8 months, the task is still difficult enough that a preference for the dominant hand is very pronounced. At 6 months, though the task is difficult, handedness has not yet fully developed, and at 10 months, though handedness has more fully developed, the task is comparatively easy and is not as pronounced.

 **CAVEATS**

While many of the babies in the study reached for the toy, not all did. And of those who reached for it, not all were able to successfully grasp and hold it. And while the majority of the babies who showed a hand preference were right-handed, your own little slugger just might be a southpaw.

 **THE TAKEAWAY**

Welcome to the world of the carrot and the stick. Expect to be dangling incentives in front of your kids for the next 18 years. From your child's perspective, this is a task that demands a significant amount of hand-eye coordination and the ability to anticipate an object's direction of movement, both skills that will help him rack up high scores on video games and win stuffed animals at carnival booths later in life. To help him further develop these skills, practice rolling and chasing balls across a floor or let him play with small mechanical toys with simple movement patterns.

I Want What You Want

Age range: 6–12 months
Experiment complexity: Simple
Research area: Social development

THE EXPERIMENT

Show your baby two similar toys. Then place the toys on a table or other surface and allow him to see you choose between the two toys. As you move your hand toward the first toy, use negative facial expressions to show that you're not interested in it—such as by wrinkling your nose and shaking your head no. Then, as you move your hand toward the second toy, use positive facial expressions to show that you're interested in it—such as a smile and raised eyebrows—and pick it up and play with it for a moment. Then return the toy to its original position and allow your child to choose one of the two toys himself.

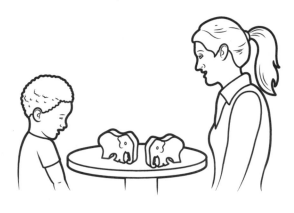

THE HYPOTHESIS

Your baby will select the same toy you chose.

TWEAK IT

As in the experiment just described, show your baby two toys, but instead of reaching out and grasping one of the toys—a clearly goal-oriented action—merely touch the toy with the back of your hand, without any attempt to grasp or retrieve it. Then allow your baby to select one of the toys.

THE RESEARCH

In a 2008 study, a group of 7-month-olds watched an adult choose one of two toys and were then given the opportunity to choose one of the toys themselves. The researchers noted that 58 percent chose the same toy the adult chose; 35 percent chose the other toy; and 7 percent made no choice.

The researchers then modified the experiment. An adult expressed interest in one of the two toys and tried to grasp it, but it was out of reach. Babies who witnessed the adult unsuccessfully reach for the toy were even more likely to select that same toy than those who witnessed the adult successfully grasp the toy—66 percent chose the toy the adult reached for, while 34 percent chose the other toy.

The study found that babies will try to reproduce actions that they perceive to be goal oriented (such as choosing a toy). However, with actions that weren't perceived to be goal oriented (such as when an adult merely touched the toy with the back of the hand, without grasping it), the babies showed no preference for the toy the adult touched.

This research suggests that babies as young as 7 months old are able to differentiate between goal-oriented actions and non-goal-oriented actions, and that they will base their own goals on the perceived goals of others.

 **THE TAKEAWAY**

The scientific community has a highly technical term for the phenomenon you likely just observed in this experiment: *Monkey see, monkey do.* From a very early age, your child takes cues from your behavior, so make sure your own goals are goals that you would want your child to emulate. Remember: You're a role model now. If you'd like to see just how much of an effect your goals and choices have, try repeating the experiment at the dinner table. When introducing a new food, let your child see you select the new food instead of a familiar food and see whether he follows your lead.

Be Still, My Face

Age range: 6–24 months
Experiment complexity: Moderate
Research area: Emotional development and social development

Note to parents: In the original experiment, babies were allowed to grow upset and cry briefly before being comforted. I recommend, however, that you end the experiment at the first sign of distress—or, if you're uncomfortable with conducting the experiment yourself, you can view a recording of it online at www.experimentingwithbabies.com/stillface.html.

 THE EXPERIMENT

Have your baby sit in a high chair or other safe place and spend a minute engaging with him: smile, sing, talk, and play. Then turn your head away briefly, and when you turn back, gaze at your baby with a neutral expression and do not engage with him.

 THE HYPOTHESIS

Your baby may make some attempts to engage with you by smiling, babbling, reaching out to you, or rapping on a tray. But he will soon become puzzled and then unnerved by your lack of response, and he may begin to frown, yawn, look away, or cry. However, once you notice your baby becoming upset, if you begin interacting with him again, he will quickly become content.

 THE RESEARCH

The "still face" experiment was first conducted in 1975 by Edward Tronick, who was researching behavioral and social development in infants. Test subjects consistently exhibited the behaviors predicted in the hypothesis. It is one of the most replicated findings in the field of developmental psychology.

This experiment demonstrates that at a young age, children have a rudimentary understanding of how social interaction works and that they are able to connect certain facial expressions with certain emotions. Subsequent studies based on the still face experiment have examined how children with conditions such as autism or hearing loss differ from their peers in the way they react to the experiment.

For instance, in a 2000 study, children with autism were found to react to the still face experiment, but only when they were already familiar with the adult participant. And in a study of deaf infants, the still face experiment was shown to have a strong effect on babies with easygoing temperaments and a less significant effect on babies with difficult temperaments.

 **THE TAKEAWAY**

A still face might be an asset at the poker table, but this experiment makes clear that your little research subject demands expressiveness. Your baby is an inherently social creature, and your facial expressions are key to his understanding your interactions with him. To help him further that understanding, make an effort to use appropriate facial expressions when you are interacting with him. For instance, it might be difficult for a young child to understand that an action such as hitting or biting has hurt you or one of his siblings. Use an expression such as a grimace or a wince to help communicate what it means to feel hurt. Similarly, when you praise your child, communicate how happy you are not only in your words but also in your expression. The still face experiment confirms that what's true for adults is also true for babies: A smile can make all the difference.

31 The In-Plain-Sight Switcheroo

Age range: 6–24 months
Experiment complexity: Simple
Research area: Cognitive development

 THE EXPERIMENT

Place two easy-to-reach containers (such as small cardboard boxes) in front of your baby. Show the baby a toy, and then place it in container A. Allow the baby to retrieve it from container A. Repeat the process several times, each time placing the toy in container A. Then place the toy in container B.

THE HYPOTHESIS

Babies younger than 1 year old will reach toward container A for the toy, even though they saw you put it in container B. By around their first birthday, babies will reach toward container B for the toy.

THE RESEARCH

The A-not-B error, also called the perseverative error, was observed in 1954 by Jean Piaget, a developmental psychologist who was studying how children come to understand object permanence. Since then, numerous other researchers have tried to tweak the experiment to determine why exactly babies make the error.

Some researchers believe that habituation—that is, repeated motor movement toward container A—causes the error, but a 1997 study suggests that more complex factors are at work. In that study, two groups of infants were tested using a version of the classic A-not-B test. They were prompted to remove the lid from an empty container A several times, then prompted to remove the lid from a container B. One group saw a toy being placed into container B before they were directed to remove the lid; the other group did not. If mere motor habituation were the cause of the A-not-B error, the results of both groups should have been the same because both were habituated to removing the lid from container A. However, the results showed that babies who saw a toy being placed in container B were less likely to make the error. The researchers acknowledge that questions remain about what exactly causes the error, but the results of their study show that motor habituation alone is an insufficient explanation.

 ## THE TAKEAWAY

Don't be so quick to laugh at your baby's error, unless you've never been fooled by a magic trick. Magicians use more sophisticated versions of this experiment—arguably a very simple form of misdirection—to fool audiences into thinking that an object has disappeared or moved from one place to another in a seemingly impossible way. If slick sleight-of-hand can baffle even you, a full-grown adult, then surely your little one should get bonus points for eventually figuring out the trick.

32 The Goldilocks Effect

Age range: 7–9 months
Experiment complexity: Complex
Research area: Cognitive development

THE EXPERIMENT

For this experiment, you'll need three rectangular pieces of cardboard, trifolded so they have a front and two sides and can stand up on a flat surface. Cover each cardboard "stand" with a distinctive color or pattern of wrapping paper, and place them side by side in front of your baby. Stand behind the display with three small toys. The toys should not resemble each other. Begin by slowly raising the first toy behind the first stand, so that it looks like the toy is peeking out at your baby. Then, lower it again. Repeat the procedure with the same toy and the same stand, keeping track of how much time elapses before your baby looks away.

On another day, repeat the experiment, but in this go-around, select a random toy and a random stand each time. Again, keep track of how much time elapses before your baby looks away.

Finally, on another day, repeat the experiment, but present the toys according to a simple sequence. For instance, you might present toy A in stand A, toy B in stand B, toy C in stand C, and then repeat the sequence. Again, keep track of how much time elapses before your baby looks away.

 **THE HYPOTHESIS**

Your baby is likely to look longer when the toys are presented in the simple sequence than in the very predictable (first) or very unpredictable (second) trials.

THE RESEARCH

Researchers have long known that babies sometimes exhibit a "familiarity bias" and sometimes exhibit a "novelty bias." In the case of the former, babies give more attention to a familiar thing than an unfamiliar thing; in the case of the latter, it's the reverse. The results of this experiment suggest one way to predict which type of bias a baby is likely to demonstrate.

In a 2012 study, 7- and 8-month-old babies were shown sequences of short animations involving recognizable objects emerging out of boxes. The predictability of the sequences was varied across trials. The researchers found that sequences of moderate predictability held infants' attention the longest, based on look-away times. The babies' attention lagged when the sequences were too predictable or when the sequences were too unpredictable.

Toward the middle is the Goldilocks point (not too easy, not too hard) at which infants' focus lasts longest. Because familiarity with a task or scenario tends to reduce its complexity, if two test stimuli are both boringly familiar, the baby will show a preference for the one closest to the Goldilocks point, which presents itself as a novelty bias. But if the two test stimuli are both unpredictable or complex, the baby will show a preference for the one closest to the Goldilocks point, which presents itself as a familiarity bias.

 **THE TAKEAWAY**

Finding your baby's sweet spot—that happy medium between "I'm bored" and "What the heck is going on here?"—can take a bit of practice. And even once you feel like you've nailed it down, expect things to shift rapidly as your baby develops. Because the limits of her attention are constantly in flux, don't get discouraged if you find she's easily distracted. She won't be confused for long.

The Importance of an Audience

Age range: 7–11 months
Experiment complexity: Simple
Research area: Social development and language development

THE EXPERIMENT

Spend about 10 minutes with your baby in unstructured playtime. Act as you normally would, but keep track of the frequency of your baby's vocalizations. Next, spend another 10 minutes playing, but this time, whenever your baby makes a vocalization, smile, move closer to your baby, and touch her. Again, keep track of the frequency of her vocalizations.

THE HYPOTHESIS

Your baby's rate of vocalization will be higher during the second 10-minute period.

THE RESEARCH

A 2003 study compared the frequency of babies' vocalizations during three back-to-back play sessions with their mothers. In the first and third play sessions, the mothers were instructed to interact as they normally would during playtime. In the second session, they were told to give positive social feedback after each of their babies' vocalizations. The researchers found that not only was the frequency of the infants' vocalizations higher during the middle session, but the sounds were more complex and had characteristics closer to mature speech—for instance, they were more fully voiced, and the number of syllables was greater.

This study shows that even at the babbling stage of language learning, the sounds that babies make are influenced by social feedback. The researchers point out that the changes in the babies' vocalizations are not the result of mere imitative behavior because the mothers' responses were nonverbal (smiling, moving closer to the infant, touching her), which calls into question theories of social learning that rely on imitation as the primary driver of developmental change.

**THE TAKEAWAY**

We've all been there: A severe case of laryngitis has threatened our ability to respond verbally with cutesy ripostes to our baby's babbling. Don't sweat it. Even nonverbal feedback, such as a flashy smile or a gentle touch can help your baby improve her language skills. Just don't go full-out mime. That's creepy.

A Gazy Connection

Age range: 9–10 months
Experiment complexity: Simple
Research area: Social development

THE EXPERIMENT

Recruit two friends to perform a brief scene in front of your baby. Have them stand side by side, facing your baby. Next, at the same time, they should turn to face each other, look into each other's eyes, and greet one another. They should then remain in that position until your baby looks away. A little while later, have the friends repeat the exchange, but this time, they should turn to face away from each other. After greeting one another, they should again remain in that position until your baby looks away.

THE HYPOTHESIS

At 10 months old, your baby will likely look longer at the exchange in which the participants are looking away from each other. But at 9 months old, there will be no significant difference in looking times.

THE RESEARCH

In a 2012 study, 9- and 10-month-old babies were shown two video clips in which two actors exchanged a greeting. In one clip, they faced away each other during the greeting, and in the other, they faced each other and gazed into each other's eyes. Only the 10-month-olds showed a difference in looking times between the two clips—they looked longer at the clip in which the actors were facing away from each other. The researchers interpreted the increase as a response to novelty (in which babies tend to look longer at unexpected things than at expected ones), which suggests that somewhere between 9 and 10 months old, babies come to expect people to look at each other during social interactions.

The fact that the 9-month-old babies failed to make a meaningful distinction between targeted gaze (in which the actors faced each other during their brief conversation) and averted gaze (in which they faced away from each other) suggests that they do not yet understand that targeted gaze is an expectation of social interaction. While they may understand that gazing at something is meaningful in certain contexts (such as when a person is reaching for an object and looks at the object as she reaches for it), they have not yet generalized their understanding of gaze to apply to social situations.

The researchers acknowledge that it's a little strange that this skill would be acquired in such a short and specific time frame, between 9 and 10 months, and they allow that a more fine-tuned experiment might show that 9-month-olds do have some degree of understanding about social gaze. However, they point out that their experiment, as designed, was simple and straightforward, and revealed a clear difference between the two groups, all of which lends weight to their conclusions.

 **THE TAKEAWAY**

Your baby is becoming a detective. She's listening in on conversations when you think she's blissfully unaware, and she's observing social interactions between other people and constantly forming hypotheses about what rules govern these interactions. Now that you know she's interested in these tête-à-têtes, give her ample opportunities to observe conversations and other social situations. That doesn't mean you have to take her to an evening cocktail party to schmooze with socialites; it could be as simple as taking her to the grocery store or letting her sit in the laps of your visiting friends while you reminisce about your preparent days.

Tools of the Trade

One classic way to determine a preverbal infant's interest level in a particular object, picture, or event is to measure his looking time. For instance, a baby might be presented with two pictures side by side, and the amount of time he spends looking at each picture during a given period might be tallied.

In earlier days, cameras were strapped to an infant's head in an attempt to indirectly measure their direction of gaze, although this technique could not measure circumstances in which the baby moved his eyes but not his head to redirect his gaze.

Nowadays, most eye-tracking systems use a technique called corneal refraction, in which near-infrared light is reflected off of the eyeball. When corneal refraction systems first became available, the subject's head had to be kept still, making it impractical for use in infant studies, but since then advances in both the eye-tracking devices and the software used for analysis have made it possible to gather accurate data in spite of infants' often erratic head movements. Indeed, it's now possible to determine not only which of two pictures a baby is looking at, but what part of the image he's focusing on.

The cutting edge of eye-tracking technology involves interpreting eye movements without the need for an infrared light source or any other special equipment, which will make eye tracking studies even simpler to produce.

Shapes or Kinds?

Age range: 10 months
Experiment complexity: Moderate
Research area: Language development

 ## THE EXPERIMENT

For this experiment, you'll need two sets of identical-looking containers, such as salt shakers or small bottles. The containers should

be opaque, so that their contents cannot be seen from the outside. With each set, fill one of the containers about halfway with salt or sugar. Into the other container, place a hard object, such as a quarter or a stone.

Present your baby with the first set of identical objects. Point to one and say, "Look! There's a wug!" Point to the other and say, "Look! There's a zav!" Then pick up each object and shake it, demonstrating the sound it makes. Make note of how long your baby looks at the objects after your demonstration.

A few days later, present your baby with the second set of identical objects. Point to each object and say, "Look! There's a fep!" Then shake each one. Again, make note of how long your baby looks at the objects after your demonstration.

 ## THE HYPOTHESIS

Your baby will spend more time looking at the objects the second time around, in which both objects were labeled with the same word, than the first time, in which the two objects were labeled with different words.

 ## THE RESEARCH

In a 2009 study, 10 month-old babies were shown two identical-looking objects that made different sounds. With one group of babies, the objects were given the same label; with another group, they were given different labels. The researchers then measured the babies' looking times after the objects were shaken.

They found that the babies looked longer when the objects were given the same label than when they were given different labels. The researchers interpreted the longer looking times to be a response to something that went against the babies' expectations. Basically, the babies had expected that objects with the same name would make the same sound, and when the objects instead made different sounds, the babies' interest was piqued, so they looked longer at the objects.

The results of the study suggest that babies use linguistic information —that is, the words used to label the objects—to predict the internal properties of objects (those unrelated to the object's appearance). Indeed, they are able to do this even if the objects are identical in appearance. The researchers point out that considering the young age of the subjects, it can be inferred that this is not a skill that is acquired at some point after the process of language acquisition has begun, but instead is present even at the very beginning of word learning.

THE TAKEAWAY

Learning which words map to which objects in a foreign tongue is an extremely difficult task for anyone, let alone someone who is still trying to get acquainted not only with a new language but with the fact that he has fingers and toes. If we were to rely only on an object's appearance for this word-mapping task, then we would be surprised to learn that a poodle and a Great Dane both share the label *dog*. But being able to group objects by other characteristics, such as the sound they make, helps resolve some of those problems. Be cognizant of this when you're helping your baby learn words that refer to things with different appearances. Help him recognize what the things have in common—their sound, their function, their wagging tails—so he can begin to form generalizations and recognize other members of a particular category, even if their appearance is unfamiliar.

36 Demonstration and Deduction

Age range: 9–15 months
Experiment complexity: Moderate
Research area: Cognitive development

 THE EXPERIMENT

On a flat surface, place a stuffed animal that is able to "hold" a small ball, and to its right, place a plastic cup that contains an identical second ball. Show your baby the objects. Wiggle the stuffed animal around for a second or two, then shake the cup to make the ball rattle inside. Now, take the objects away, remove the ball from the cup, and then put the objects back. Move your baby within reach of the objects and observe her behavior for about 60 seconds. Note whether she removes the ball from the stuffed animal, whether

she places it in the cup, and whether she shakes the cup to make the ball rattle.

A few days later, set up the objects again, but this time, leave the plastic cup empty. As your baby watches, take the ball from the stuffed animal, place it inside the cup, and shake the cup to make the ball rattle inside. Take the objects away, put the ball back to its original position, and then put the objects back. Move your baby within reach of the objects and observe her behavior for about 60 seconds. Again, note whether she removes the ball from the stuffed animal, whether she places it in the cup, and whether she shakes the cup to make the ball rattle.

 TWEAK IT

If you are able to perform the experiment on two babies of roughly the same age, you can assign one to each condition, rather than repeating the experiment a few days later. This will eliminate the possibility that your baby's familiarization with the procedure might skew the results the second time around.

 ## THE HYPOTHESIS

The first time you perform the experiment, your baby is likely to take the ball from the stuffed animal. But what she does next depends on her age. If she's on the young side, around 9 months old, she's unlikely to place the ball in the cup, although she may shake the empty cup. If she's on the older side, around 15 months, she may place the ball in the cup but is unlikely to shake it.

The second time you perform the experiment, your baby is again likely to take the ball from the stuffed animal. If she's on the young side, her behavior is unlikely to differ significantly from the first time. But if she's on the older side, she is likely to reproduce your demonstration by placing the ball in the cup and shaking it to make the ball rattle.

 ## THE RESEARCH

In a 2007 study, babies in three age groups—9, 12, and 15 months old—were tested on their ability to learn a three-step sequence. Some of the babies from each age group were placed in a "control" condition, in which they were shown the final step of the sequence (a cup being shaken, and a ball rattling inside) but not the first two steps (the ball being taken from the stuffed animal and then placed in the cup). Other babies were placed in a "demonstration" condition, in which all three steps of the sequence were demonstrated. The babies were then given an opportunity to manipulate the objects, and the researchers took note of how many of the steps each baby was able to complete.

The babies in the 9-month group took the ball from the stuffed animal but otherwise did not show much difference between the two conditions. The demonstration babies in the 12-month group were more likely than the control babies to take the ball from the stuffed animal and place it in the cup, and they exclusively shook the cup after placing the ball inside, while the control babies exclusively shook the cup while it was empty. Babies in the 15-month group performed similarly to those in the 12-month group.

The researchers concluded that at about 9 months old, babies are able to learn the first step in a sequence but don't yet have the capacity to learn the subsequent steps in the sequence. That soon changes, though. In the demonstration condition, one-third of the 12-month-olds and two-thirds of the 15-month-olds were able to reproduce all three steps in the sequence. However, in these age groups, the babies still need to have all of the steps demonstrated, as evidenced by the fact that none of the babies in the control condition were able to spontaneously perform the sequence. Thus the researchers concluded that by 15 months, babies are able to learn and reproduce the steps in a three-step sequence, but they are not yet able to infer an intermediate step that has not been demonstrated.

 **THE TAKEAWAY**

Your baby might not yet have enough understanding about cause and effect to be able to deduce the steps required to reach a goal, but this study shows that if each of those steps is demonstrated, she may be able to learn and reproduce the sequence. You can help her learn by being very deliberate and methodical when you model a new skill, such as pressing a certain button to turn on a toy and another button to make it play music. Think about all of the steps that the sequence requires, and make sure she sees you perform each step in turn.

37 Defending What's Mine

Age range: 9–24 months
Experiment complexity: Simple
Research area: Social development

THE EXPERIMENT

Arrange a play date for your baby with a child who is about the same age. Select some toys that both babies are likely to be interested in and allow them to play with the toys for about 20 minutes. Both you and the parent of the other child should remain in the room and interact naturally with the children, but for the most part, try to let them play without interference or coaching. Pay special attention to any instances in which one child takes a toy that the other is playing with or has just put down. Note

how the other child reacts to the toy being taken away from him: Does he resist, by reaching for the toy and trying to pull it back? Does he cry or use words to protest the toy being taken away? Does he show aggressive behavior (for example, pushing or striking the other child)?

 ## THE HYPOTHESIS

The likelihood of either child reacting in any of these ways to a toy being taken away will vary with age. Children between 9 and 12 months old are significantly more likely to demonstrate resisting behavior than aggressive behavior and very unlikely to use crying or vocalizations as a means of protesting the action. But by 24 months old, children are about as likely to demonstrate resisting and aggressive behavior and much more likely to use crying or vocalizations.

 THE RESEARCH

A 2011 study examined the behaviors of children ranging from 9 months old to 30 months old as they interacted with children of roughly the same age. In the majority of play sessions, there was at least one instance of a "takeover," in which a child picked up a toy that another child was playing with or had recently put down. A minority of children in each age group exhibited negative reactions to their toy being taken away, although the percentage became larger with age. At both 12 months and 24 months old, about 10 percent of children who exhibited such a response used aggression; by 30 months, almost 40 percent did. Crying and vocal protests also rose with age, while resisting behavior decreased with age.

The results of this study show that the use of physical force in response to a toy being taken away by a peer emerges around 12 months, although it is exhibited by only a minority of babies. The researchers note that the use of words such as *Mine!*—which emerges around age 2—demonstrates that toddlers have already come to learn that it can be useful to make claims on toys. And an analysis of the data that differentiated responses by gender found that boys are more likely to use aggressive protests and girls are more likely to use vocal protests, even though they're both about as likely to object to the toys being taken away.

 **THE TAKEAWAY**

Whether your child remains composed after a toy takeover will, of course, depend on factors like general temperament, age, and gender. More important is *your* reaction. If he hits or is otherwise aggressive to the other child, step in and break up the baby scuffle, and if possible, deliver a little discourse on the importance of sharing. If he's old enough for a time-out to have disciplinary value, it can help reinforce that such behavior is not acceptable. If he's still too young to learn anything from a time-out, then removing him from the situation will still protect his playmate and give him a chance to calm down.

Don't Try This at Home

In the mid-1950s, Congress passed a law requiring that safety and prevention measures be devised to minimize the risk of children getting trapped inside refrigerators.

As a response to that law, the journal *Pediatrics* published "Behavior of Young Children Under Conditions Simulating Entrapment in Refrigerators," a study that—you guessed it—placed children ages 2 to 5 inside a refrigerator-like box and observed whether they could escape. About a quarter of the kids escaped in fewer than 10 seconds, and about three quarters escaped (or were released) within three minutes.

Among the metrics studied: Success of escape based on the child's age, size, and behavior; force exerted; time spent inside the box; and whether the child cried out for help.

Based on the data from this study, new standards were created for release devices within refrigerators, and for decades, refrigerator manufacturers have been required by federal law to conform to these standards.

A follow-up study eight months later assessed the children to see whether the study had caused any long-term psychological damage, such as reversion to infantile behavior. Fortunately, no children appeared to have been permanently scarred by the experience, although, according to the researchers who conducted the follow-up study, "a number of children still talked about the tests, some with pleasure, a few with resentment."

Taking Cues

Age range: 10–12 months
Experiment complexity: Moderate
Research area: Emotional development

 THE EXPERIMENT

Select four ordinary household objects of about the same size that your baby will be interested in touching but that are not at all harmful or threatening, such as a ball of yarn, a pack of playing cards, or a small plastic mug. They should be items that your baby has never played with before.

Secure your baby in a high chair or car seat and place two of the items in front of her, out of reach. Stand behind the objects, facing your baby, and direct your gaze at one of the objects. Say, "Look at that." Then spend about 15 seconds describing the object using a neutral facial expression and neutral voice. (For instance, in

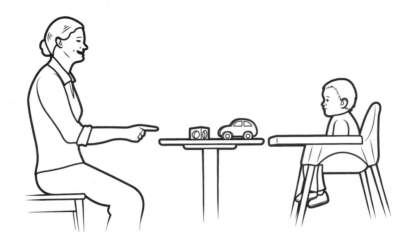

the case of the mug, you might say, "It's plastic. It's red. It has a handle.") Finally, say, "Look at that" again. Then move both objects within your baby's reach, and give her about 30 seconds to play with them. Note which object she is more interested in.

Now you'll repeat the presentation with the other two objects, but this time, instead of a neutral facial expression and neutral voice, you should use a fearful facial expression and negative tone of voice (begin with a gasp and continue with tense, rapidly spoken words). Even though your facial and vocal cues will be negative, during your description of the object, avoid negatively charged words such as *ugly* or *scary*. Instead, use factual, descriptive words. Then move both objects within your baby's reach and give her about 30 seconds to play with them. Note which object she is more interested in.

THE HYPOTHESIS

Ten-month-olds will not show a preference for either object in either of the presentations. Twelve-month-olds, however, will gravitate toward the described object after the neutral presentation, but will avoid the described object after the negative presentation.

THE RESEARCH

In a 2003 study, 10- and 12-month-old babies watched video presentations in which an actress directed her attention to one of two objects in front of her and referred to the object using a neutral tone and expression. The babies were then able to play with the objects. Then half the babies were shown a similar presentation, but in this one, the actress took on a negative (fearful) tone and expression. The other half saw a presentation in which the actress took on a positive (enthusiastic) tone and expression. They were then permitted to play with the new set of objects.

The researchers found that the 10-month-olds didn't show any significant difference in their response to any of the three conditions (neutral, negative, and positive). But the 12-month-olds were more likely to reach for the target object than the other object after the neutral and positive presentations and less likely to reach for the target object after the negative presentation. They were also more likely to adopt a negative state themselves.

The researchers concluded that the 12-month-olds were able to take cues from the actress's expression and tone of voice and apply those cues to the specific object she was talking about, while the 10-month-olds had not yet acquired that ability.

 **THE TAKEAWAY**

Being able to pick up on other people's emotional cues is a fantastically useful skill. It can prevent you from unintentionally starting a bar fight. It can help you understand that if you walk into your boss's office and find him weeping uncontrollably, you probably shouldn't ask him for a raise at that very moment. It can also keep you out of danger, and that's especially important for vulnerable little babies. By picking up on a fearful emotional state, they're learning to avoid an object that could potentially harm them. This is about the time in their development, then, when you can point to dangerous things—the stovetop, the knife drawer, anybody with a face tattoo— and warn them to stay away.

Walking Tour

Age range: 10–16 months
Experiment complexity: Moderate
Research area: Motor skills

 THE EXPERIMENT

Conduct this experiment once your baby is walking independently. During a warm day, place a sheet of butcher paper about 12 feet long on a level outdoor surface and apply nonpermanent ink to her feet so that the toes and the heel of each foot are clearly marked. (If you'd rather do this experiment

indoors, dip her feet in water instead, to avoid making a mess.) Next, encourage her to walk across the paper to you. Then, repeat the process with your own feet, and walk normally over another sheet of butcher paper, several feet longer than the one you used for her. Now, examine the footprints that she and you left behind on the butcher paper. You can repeat this experiment several times, over the course of months or even years, to watch for changes in her walking pattern.

THE HYPOTHESIS

Shortly after your baby begins walking independently, step width (the distance between the left foot and right foot while you walk) will be about 25 percent shorter for you than for her, although chubbier bodies in both infants and adults will have wider step widths. In addition, your left and right feet will be nearly parallel, but hers will be turned out, possibly by as much as 40 percent. Your walking pattern will be much straighter than hers, and even accounting for leg length, her step lengths will be smaller than yours.

THE RESEARCH

The development of walking skills has been extensively studied, with a focus on when and how walking begins and progresses. A 2009 study attempted to build on this body of research by trying to determine why walking improves. Specifically, researchers examined whether improvements in walking skills can be attributed to developmental maturation, practice, or changes in body type. They studied the walking patterns of babies, kindergarteners, and adults using the technique described above, in which inked tabs were placed on the subjects' shoes. They found differences in step length beyond that which would be explained by accounting for leg length, step width, foot rotation (whether toes point in or out), and dynamic base, a measure of the straightness of walking determined by calculating the angle of three consecutive steps. They then looked for correlations between these differences and the subjects' ages, amount of practice walking, and body types. They found that a baby's amount of practice walking, which could be roughly measured by calculating the time since the baby started walking, had a large effect: Babies with the most practice had walking patterns more similar to adult walking patterns. Age and changing body types, on the other hand, had little effect on their own.

The study's authors note that walking researchers in earlier decades had considered age, an indirect measure of brain maturation, to be the most important factor in walking improvements. But since the 1980s, researchers have focused more on their subjects' level of walking experience. The results of this study confirm that walking experience is indeed the more salient factor. They point out that in the course of a normal day, independent walkers might take thousands of steps across a variety of different terrains—carpet, tile, hardwood, grass, concrete—and each is a new opportunity to refine their walking technique.

THE TAKEAWAY

Walking is an activity that your baby will need little encouragement to practice, once she gets the hang of it. Expect her to zoom around whatever area she's allowed to explore, whether it's a tiny room or a wide-open space. During the times when she's bouncing off the walls, it's good to remember that, as with many other aspects of child development, the amount of practice your child gets will have the biggest impact on her progress. So, though it may be faster (and less dizzying) to get from Point A to Point B with her in your arms, try to give preference to letting her walk on her own.

Familiarity and Foods

Age range: 12 months
Experiment complexity: Moderate
Research area: Social development

THE EXPERIMENT

Recruit two friends, including one who speaks a foreign language, to help you with this experiment. Prepare two sweet foods, such as applesauce and pureed apricots, and place each in a separate bowl. Have your English-speaking friend hold one of the bowls, smile, and say to your baby, "This is one of my favorite foods to eat." Then, have your friend taste a spoonful of the food and say, "Yummy!" Next, with a baby spoon, offer some of the food to your child. Now, direct your other friend to do the same thing with the other bowl, but speaking in a foreign language. Then, offer some of the second food

to your child. Finally, both of the friends should simultaneously offer their bowls to your baby.

THE HYPOTHESIS

Your baby will choose the bowl of food offered by the English-speaking friend.

THE RESEARCH

Babies have pretty low standards about the things they'll put in their mouth: They tend to follow the "if it fits in there, I'll try it" diet. It might, at first blush, seem strange that natural selection hasn't given them more discriminating eating habits—after all, you eat something toxic as an infant and you won't be around to reproduce. But bear in mind that in the early years of life, humans depend on others to feed them, and so they don't really have to deal with the problem of food selection; their foods are selected for them. Indeed, this sometimes works to parents' advantage because at 12 months a baby will be willing to try veggies that a year later he'll refuse to touch.

A 2009 study tested 12-month-old babies for whom English was the primary language spoken at home. The babies watched as two women each presented a food choice. One woman spoke English; the other spoke French. Both tasted and expressed delight with the foods, and most of the babies tried each food when it was individually presented to them. But when the babies were given a choice between the two foods, a majority, about 60 percent, chose the food that had been associated with the English-speaking woman, while only about 25 percent chose the food that had been associated with the French-speaking woman. (The experimenters controlled for conditions such as which language was spoken by the woman, which food was associated with the woman, and which order the languages were presented.)

The babies in the study used language familiarity as a social cue that either imparted a preference where no preference existed or overruled an only slightly developed preference based on taste. The study offers evidence that the earliest expressions of food preference use these social cues as a bridge between the very low discrimination shown before a child reaches his first birthday, and the more refined preferences, based on the qualities of the food itself, that emerge later.

 **THE TAKEAWAY**

Savor these moments, in which subtle social cues can persuade your baby to try the vegetables on his plate. In but a few short years, neither heaven nor earth will be able to convince him. In the meantime, try to expose him to the widest variety of foods you can. As for your baby's preference for native speakers, it's a normal part of his language development, not evidence of xenophobia. In fact, because babies and young children are much better at picking up new languages than we adults are, now's a great time to expose him to a foreign tongue, particularly because multilingual workers are likely to be in even higher demand by the time your baby reaches adulthood.

The Retriever

Age range: 11–13 months
Experiment complexity: Simple
Research area: Motor skills

 THE EXPERIMENT

Conduct this experiment around 11 months, or when your baby is an experienced crawler but not yet a walker. During a long session of uninterrupted playtime with your baby (an hour or more), observe the way he interacts with objects. If he crawls to an object across the room, does he play with it or share it while remaining in the place where it was discovered, or does he retrieve it by crawling back to you to play with it or share it?

THE HYPOTHESIS

The more your baby retrieves—that is, he crawls to a distant object, then crawls back with the object in hand—and the more he shares the retrieved object, the more likely he is to walk by 13 months.

THE RESEARCH

In a 2011 study, researchers observed a group of 11-month-old experienced crawlers, none of whom had begun walking yet, during unstructured playtime with their mothers in a home setting. The researchers returned to the homes two months later and again observed the babies, about half of whom had begun walking. They found that the babies who were walkers at 13 months had been more likely, at 11 months, to crawl to distant objects, carry objects, and share objects with their mothers. For instance, the walkers had, at 11 months, crawled to distant objects about twice as frequently as the nonwalkers had. They had also carried objects nearly five times as much as the nonwalkers had. And although only a small number of infants (about 15 percent) exhibited retrieval behavior, nearly all of the ones who did were walking two months later.

The researchers noted that once the infants did begin to walk, their willingness to pursue distant objects and to carry objects increased substantially—which stands to reason because walking enables them to get places faster and to have their hands free to carry things. They concluded that the desire to do these things at 11 months is likely to motivate the babies to begin walking sooner.

THE TAKEAWAY

You may be eagerly hoping that your baby turns out to be an early walker. Or—especially if this isn't your first child—you might be dreading the day he becomes bipedal and able to zoom away even faster. In either case, if you see him acting like a golden retriever during playtime, you'd better charge up those camera batteries. His first step is likely on its way soon!

Tools of the Trade

One high-tech method researchers use to determine a baby's response to an image, sound, or other stimulus is to measure her brain's electrical activity by placing electrodes on her scalp, a process called electroencephalography (EEG).

For instance, in one recent study, EEG data were collected during an experiment in which 7-month-old babies were shown a photograph of a woman's face accompanied by the sound of her voice.

An analysis of the EEG data found that when the photo and the voice conveyed the same emotion (such as a smiling face and a cheerful tone of voice), it produced one type of brain wave, and when the photo and the voice conveyed different emotions (such as a smiling face and an angry tone of voice), it produced a different type of brain wave.

42 # I Know Something You Don't Know

Age range: 13–15 months
Experiment complexity: Moderate
Research area: Cognitive development

 ## THE EXPERIMENT

Place two same-size boxes on a table in front of your baby, with their openings facing each other, and place a small toy between

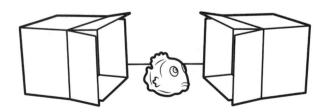

them. Direct a friend to walk up to the toy, play with it briefly, then place it into one of the boxes, pausing with her hand in the box for a second or two before withdrawing it. Next, have the friend walk away briefly, then return and place her hand in the box with the toy in it for a few seconds. She should then withdraw her hand, leaving the toy inside. Now, have the friend leave the room. While she is out of the room, allow your baby to see you move the toy to the other box. Now, direct your friend to return to the room. Without looking into either of the boxes, she should reach into the one that previously contained the toy, and keep her hand inside the box for several seconds. Observe your baby's reaction to her choice. A few days later, repeat the experiment, but this time, your friend should reach into the *other* box—the one that actually does contain the toy.

 ## THE HYPOTHESIS

The second time you perform the experiment, your baby will be surprised that your friend reached into the box that now contains the toy because he doesn't expect your friend to know that the toy has been moved. Because he is surprised, he will look at your friend's final pose longer this time than he did the first time, when the friend reached, as expected, into the box where she had left the toy.

 **TWEAK IT**

If you are able to perform the experiment on two babies of roughly the same age, you can assign one to each condition, rather than repeating the experiment a few days later. This will eliminate the possibility that your baby's familiarization with the procedure might skew the results the second time around.

 THE RESEARCH

In a 2005 study, 15-month-old babies were presented with a scenario much like the one described above. They looked significantly longer—almost 10 seconds more, on average—when the adult reached into the box that contained the toy than when the adult reached into the box that no longer contained the toy. A similar 2007 study found that babies as young as 13 months old also demonstrated surprise when an animated character made a choice about the location of an object that was inconsistent with the information available to the character.

Whether babies are able to understand the belief states of other people—that is, whether they can keep track of what true or false beliefs other people hold—has been a point of contention among psychology researchers. In a number of previous experiments, children did not demonstrate that they could recognize the false beliefs of others until they were 3 or 4 years old. But the researchers who designed the 2005 study sought to eliminate aspects of those previous experiments that may have inhibited younger children. They purposefully constructed a sequence that was entirely nonverbal and relatively simple in its presentation.

The researchers concluded that the babies were able to grasp that the adult understood the toy to be in the first box, even though it was actually in the second box. They expected the adult to reach into the box that ostensibly contained the toy (the first box), and so it violated their expectation when the adult instead reached into the second box.

The results of this study suggest that an understanding of the belief states of other people is present at an age far earlier than what previous experiments had suggested. The researchers note that the study may lead to further developments in two particular areas of psychological research. The first is atypical development because previous experiments have shown that autistic children do poorly on false-belief tests. The second is animal cognition, for which an entirely nonverbal experiment might be useful to help determine whether animals are able to understand the belief states of people.

 **THE TAKEAWAY**

Your little ragamuffin is a mind reader, at least in a rudimentary way. He is able to separate the facts that he knows from the facts that he thinks you know, and he sets expectations based on that knowledge. Being able to keep track of what other people know is a terrific developmental skill, because it allows us to make sense of their behavior. For instance, we may know that a hungry wolf has disguised himself as Little Red Riding Hood's grandmother, but if we also know that Little Red Riding Hood is unaware of this, then we can understand why she would enter the house and address the wolf as if it were her grandmother. There's little you can do to speed up your baby's acquisition of this skill, but through experiments such as the one described here, you can determine whether it has been acquired. Once he's reached a point at which he seems to understand the extent of other people's knowledge, you can continue to devise little experiments to test just how much he knows. You may be surprised to learn that he knows more than you think!

43 Using Your Head

Age range: 13–15 months
Experiment complexity: Moderate
Research area: Motor skills

 THE EXPERIMENT

For this experiment, you'll need an object that you can activate by touching it with your forehead, such as a small dome style light or a toy that makes noise or lights up when it's touched. Sit at a table opposite your baby and place the object in front of you. Raise your hands in the air, then get your baby's attention by saying his name. With arms still in the air, lower your forehead to touch the object and activate its light or sound. Repeat the procedure several times, then ask your baby if he wants to try. Place the object in front of him so that he can also activate it if he touches it with his forehead. Observe whether he attempts to imitate you.

A few days later, repeat the experiment, but this time, don't put your arms in the air. Instead, place your hands on the table, so that your baby can see that you *could* tap the object with your hands if you wanted to, but that you are purposely using your head instead.

THE HYPOTHESIS

The first time you conduct the experiment, your baby is unlikely to touch the object with his forehead. If he does make an attempt, he is unlikely to put his hands in the air as he does so. The second time you conduct the experiment, your baby will be more likely to imitate your action—that is, touching the object with his forehead, with his hands on the table.

THE RESEARCH

In a 2011 study, 14-month-old babies were split up into several groups. Each group was shown the forehead-touch action but with slight variations in the method demonstrated. For instance, in one group, the person who demonstrated the action had her hands free; in another, her hands were raised in the air; in another, her hands were not visible and presumably occupied; and in another, her hands were holding small balls but were otherwise able to tap the object. The researchers found that babies in the hands-free group were twice as likely to imitate the action as those in the hands-in-air group.

The same results had been seen in a similar study nine years earlier. In that study, the researchers theorized that the babies in the hands-free condition assumed the person demonstrating the action had a good reason for touching the object with her head, even though her hands were free to touch it, and thus they were more willing to use the same head-touch method when imitating the action. In contrast, the babies in the hands-occupied condition assumed that because her hands were not free to touch the object, she had no choice but to use her head to touch it instead. The authors thus concluded that babies are able to take into account the rationale behind an action when imitating it.

But the researchers in 2011 put forth an alternate explanation: It is the baby's existing motor skills, rather than the rationale behind the action, that has the stronger effect on imitation. The results of their study support that explanation. In both the hands-free and hands-in-air conditions, the demonstrator's hands were ostensibly available to touch the object. But in the hands-free condition, the action was closer to the babies' existing repertoire of motor skills than in the hands-in-air condition. In fact, the researchers note, even among the babies in the hands-in-air group who did touch the object with their heads, not a single one did so with their hands in the air. Thus they concluded that a baby's degree of familiarity with a particular motor skill—what the researchers call *motor resonance*—has a bigger effect on imitation than the rationality of the action.

 ## THE TAKEAWAY

Here's a case in which two very plausible reasons for a baby's behavior have been put forth, but only one is the true explanation. You'll likely find that in your daily interactions with your child, you'll encounter many instances in which such dueling hypotheses occur. Perhaps one parent thinks baby's not napping well because he's uncomfortable, and the other parent thinks he's not tired. Or maybe you're not sure whether your baby's eating lint off the floor because he's hungry or just a clean freak. Sometimes, it's simply impossible to know for sure, and other times it only takes a different perspective to see what is really going on. So if you're stumped, don't be afraid to ask around. Your pediatrician, your friends, and even your other children may be able to offer some compelling arguments.

A Questioning Look

Age range: 13–18 months
Experiment complexity: Moderate
Research area: Cognitive development and social development

THE EXPERIMENT

Select three small objects that are safe for your baby to hold and manipulate. Try to choose objects whose names your baby would not recognize, such as a pedometer, a trivet, or a knickknack. Place your baby into a high chair or other seat. On a table or other flat surface in front of her, place one of the objects to her left and one to her right, both out of her reach. Now, have a friend sit in front of your baby, so that the objects are between your baby and your friend. The friend should stare at the center of the table, so that his eyes are not fixed toward either of the two objects, and say, "Look at the toma! There's the toma. Do you see the toma?" Then, he should

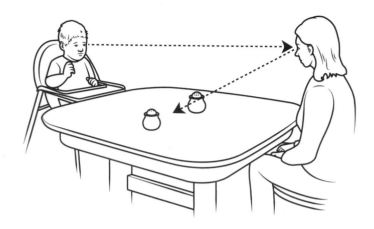

spend about 10 more seconds staring at the center of the table while you observe your baby. Be on the lookout for how many times your baby glances at the friend during that time, and for how long.

Some time later, repeat the experiment, but this time use only the third object. Place it in either the left position or right position and leave the other position empty. Your friend should follow the same procedure, but this time, have him label the object a "modi." Again, watch how many times your baby glances at the friend afterward.

 ## THE HYPOTHESIS

Your baby will glance at the friend more often when there are two objects on the table than when there is only one.

 **THE RESEARCH**

In a 2011 study of 13- and 18-month-old babies, half of the babies in each age group were assigned to the two-object condition, and the other half were assigned to the one-object condition. The researchers wanted to see how the babies in the two-object condition would attempt to resolve the ambiguity they were presented with: one word that could refer to either of the two objects. They found that the babies looked to the experimenter for clarification more frequently than did the babies in the one-object condition, who appeared to be able to connect the label with the single object and thus had less of a need for clarification. Presumably, the babies in the two-object condition were trying to figure out which of the objects the experimenter was looking at, which would help them determine which object the experimenter was referring to.

What's fascinating about the results of this experiment, the researchers point out, is that the babies in the two-objects condition were able to understand that an ambiguity existed and that they needed more information to resolve the ambiguity. In addition, they knew to look to the experimenter in an attempt to get more information. The findings have implications for researchers who study language acquisition. Specifically, they indicate that babies as young as 13 months old rely on social cues, such as the direction of a person's gaze toward an object, to resolve ambiguities when learning new words.

 **THE TAKEAWAY**

You are your baby's Google. Now that you know your baby will actively look to you in situations in which she needs more information, you can be on the lookout for them and respond accordingly. For instance, if you tell her to "go get the ball" or "pick up the toy" and you get an uncertain glance in response, you might want to look at the object to which you are referring and point to it for reinforcement.

Power Napping

Age range: 15 months
Experiment complexity: Complex
Research area: Language development

 ## THE EXPERIMENT

Start the first part of this experiment before a scheduled nap. Your goal is to familiarize your baby with a language pattern in which words are bookended by the same set of nonsense syllables. The prefix for each word will be *pel*, and the suffix will be *rud*. So, for instance, you might recite the following words to your baby:

> *Pel-ladder-rud. Pel-coffee-rud. Pel-giraffe-rud. Pel-soda-rud. Pel-armchair-rud.*

Continue with the recitation, using the same pattern, until you've rattled off about 30 words.

Conduct the second stage of the experiment after your baby takes a nap. Capture your baby's attention and start a timer. Begin reciting one of the following test sets of words and stop the timer when she looks away.

Familiar Test Set

In this test set, you'll use the same two nonsense syllables you used in the first part of the experiment (*pel* as prefix and *rud* as suffix). Feel free to use the example words below, or make up your own.

> *Pel-pickle-rud. Pel-truck-rud. Pel-Vermont-rud. Pel-joyful-rud. Pel-sleet-rud. Pel-after-rud.*

Unfamiliar Test Set

In this test set, you'll use a different pattern of nonsense syllables. For some words, use *jic* as a prefix and *rud* as a suffix, and for other words, use *pel* as a prefix and *vot* as a suffix. Feel free to use the example words below, or make up your own.

> *Jic-random-rud. Pel-pucker-vot. Jic-candy-rud. Pel-woman-vot. Jic-lake-rud. Pel-into-vot.*

Repeat the process several times, alternating both test sets.

THE HYPOTHESIS

Examine your baby's looking times—starting from when you capture her attention and begin reciting a test set and ending when she looks away. She is likely to show little difference in looking times between the two test sets. However, if she does show a preference, it will probably be for whichever test set came first.

THE RESEARCH

A 2006 study examined whether napping enhances a baby's ability to figure out patterns that occur in language. During the study's familiarization stage, babies were exposed to a set of nonsense words that shared a common construct: They began with one of two syllables (such as *pel*), and each of those beginning syllables had a corresponding ending syllable (such as *rud*).

Four hours later, the test stage was conducted. The researchers conducted the study in such a way that for about half of the babies, that four-hour stretch would fall during their regular naptime, and for the other half, it would be during a period when the babies did not regularly nap.

The babies who napped showed no looking-time preference between the familiar and unfamiliar test sets. The babies who did not nap, on the other hand, showed a significant preference for the familiar test set.

The researchers theorize that the babies who napped had been able to generalize the rules that governed the construction of the nonsense words, and thus they showed little distinction in their responses to the familiar and unfamiliar test sets. To the nappers, each of the words in both test sets followed the same general rule: a root word with a prefix that was associated with a particular suffix. Thus, in a sense, even the unfamiliar words were familiar because they followed the same language rule.

The non-nappers, on the other hand, were able to retain the specific test words in their memory over a four-hour period—no small task!—but apparently were not able to form a generalization about the structure of the nonsense words. Thus there was nothing familiar to them about the unfamiliar test set, and so they showed a preference for the words they recognized rather than words they had never heard before.

 THE TAKEAWAY

It's the goal of every hard-partying college student: to find a way to nap *and* study at the same time. Turns out, in babies, that's exactly what's happening. Though we don't know exactly how napping causes the language generalization demonstrated in the study, it's obvious that sleep is a key part of the process. Fortunately, at least in this case, everyone's best interests are aligned: No parent in her right mind is going to object to her baby taking a good, long nap—and, it turns out, the nap not only will rejuvenate her baby and put her in better spirits but also will help her acquire language. A little snooze may also enhance postnap learning. A 2011 study found that, at least in adults, the ability to commit things to memory improves after a nap. If that holds true for babies as well, then the period directly after a nap is a great time to expose your baby to new words and content-rich activities, such as reading and singing.

46 Same or Similar?

Age range: 14–20 months
Experiment complexity: Moderate
Research area: Language development

THE EXPERIMENT

Alternately show your baby two toys or other objects that are dissimilar in appearance. When you show the first toy, call it "bih," using a slightly drawn-out, descending intonation for emphasis. Then show the second toy, and call it "dih." Repeat the presentations somewhere between 10 and 20 times, until your baby starts to lose interest. Then, after a brief interlude, present the first toy again, but call it "dih."

THE HYPOTHESIS

At 20 months, your baby will look longer at the toy the second time you showed it to him than he did the first time. But at 14 months, he is not likely to look longer.

THE RESEARCH

A 2002 study attempted to determine at what age babies are able to distinguish between similar-sounding words when they are used to label objects. They familiarized their 20-month-old test subjects with two nonsense words, "bih" and "dih," that were used to label two toys. Then, for half of the babies, they presented one of the toys and used the familiar label. For the other half, they presented the toy but used the label that had been used with the other toy. They found that those who heard the unfamiliar label looked longer at the toy than those who heard the familiar label, which indicated that the former group had been able to distinguish between the two words and were surprised to hear the wrong label applied. The researchers then conducted the same experiment with 14- and 17-month-olds. The 14-month-olds did not appear to be able to distinguish between the two words, based on their looking times, but the 17-month-olds were able to make the distinction.

Language-acquisition researchers have observed that at or around 18 months, babies become significantly better at learning new words and undergo a "naming explosion," at which point they pick up words so quickly it becomes almost impossible for parents to make an accurate inventory of the words their baby can understand. Yet even though babies as young as 8 months old can distinguish between similar-sounding syllables, it takes much longer for them to distinguish between similar-sounding words when they are used to label objects. To determine at what point babies are able to make this distinction, this study examined babies who were several months away from the naming explosion, babies who were on the cusp of it, and babies who were a couple of months past the acceleration point. That the 14-month-olds did not distinguish between the nonsense words but the older babies did suggests that there is only a brief window of time when babies confuse similar-sounding words as they try to learn them.

The researchers also found that in all the age groups, babies with larger-than-average vocabulary sizes were best at distinguishing between the similar-sounding words. The researchers suggest two explanations for the correlation between vocabulary size and word-discrimination ability among the early word learners. One theory is that as vocabulary size increases, the likelihood of acquiring similar-sounding words increases, so the baby is forced to better distinguish between words. Another theory is that babies who are farther along in the word-acquisition process are able to devote more attention to subtle sound distinctions because picking up new words is not as taxing as it had been earlier in the process. This is the theory the researchers prefer, and they point out that it is consistent with earlier studies that suggest that when babies are faced with tasks that demand significant focus and brainpower, they are less able to pay attention to more subtle details.

 **THE TAKEAWAY**

It may seem like your baby leads a carefree life—he has devoted servants who feed him, clothe him, bathe him and entertain him—but make no mistake: His brain is working hard, and picking up a language with no formal instruction is not an easy task. Particularly in the early months of his word learning, the intense effort it takes his brain to acquire new words may lead him to confuse similar-sounding words. But that phase will soon pass, and he'll enter into a phase where similar-sounding words are not only easy to distinguish but also delightful to the ear. (No wonder Dr. Seuss's rhyming verses are so popular.) In the meantime, let your baby's brain work at its own natural pace.

The Ambiguous "One"

Age range: 16–18 months
Experiment complexity: Moderate
Research area: Language development

THE EXPERIMENT

Conduct this experiment around the time when your baby begins using two-word phrases. By this point in their language development, babies have come to understand that words can be strung together according to certain grammar rules.

Gather two objects that differ in color but are of the same kind, such as two bottles, two rattles, or two balls. Show your baby one of the objects, and identify it. For instance, you might say, "Look! A yellow ball." Repeat this presentation once or twice, then remove the object from view. Next, display both objects at the same time, one in your left hand and one in your right hand. Say, "Now look.

Do you see another one?" Make note of which object he looks at, and for how long.

 THE HYPOTHESIS

Your baby will look longer at the object you presented earlier.

 THE RESEARCH

This is one of those experiments for which the hypothesis seems pretty simple and obvious, but it has intriguing and wide-reaching implications for language-development researchers.

First, some background: In the 1950s and 1960s, now-legendary linguist Noam Chomsky formulated theories about how language is structured, how we comprehend it, and how we come to acquire it. He argued that certain rules of language are hardwired into the human brain—that is, they are not simply acquired through experience. Detractors argue that children can pick up everything they need to know about language from the speech they hear around them.

In a 2003 study, three language-development researchers devised an experiment to test whether babies are able to pick up on an aspect of English grammar that, they argue, the babies could not have learned simply by listening to speech in their environment because it doesn't occur frequently enough. They presented an object that was described with an adjective-noun phrase (*yellow ball*). Then, they presented two objects, both of which fit the noun (*ball*) but only one of which matched the adjective-noun phrase. They asked the babies, "Do you see another one?"

The researchers argued that if the babies understood *one* to refer to only the noun, they would not show a preference for either of the two objects because both matched the noun. But if they understood *one* to refer to the adjective-noun phrase, as adults do, they would show a preference for the object that matched that phrase. As it turns out, the babies did show a preference for the object that matched the adjective-noun phrase.

This finding lends support to the idea that this particular language rule is innate, rather than acquired, knowledge. It's a big win for Chomsky lovers.

 **THE TAKEAWAY**

Chomsky wasn't the first to argue that we're born with innate knowledge. Great philosophers like Plato, Descartes, and Leibniz also put forth variations on the idea. (Another great philosopher, John Locke, famously disagreed, arguing that the mind begins as a tabula rasa, or clean slate.) But Chomsky certainly did set off an explosion of research in the field of child development that deals with whether some knowledge is innate rather than acquired. Over the past several decades, studies have shown that babies appear to have an inborn concept of not only grammar but also rudimentary mathematics and physics. These core concepts that are prewired in your baby enhance his ability to make sense of the world. So in your daily interactions with him, don't hesitate to expose him to unfamiliar words, actions, and situations. They may not be so unfamiliar after all.

48 Helping the Helper

Age range: 18–24 months
Experiment complexity: Moderate
Research area: Social development and behavioral development

THE EXPERIMENT

Enlist the help of two adult friends. Have one friend show your toddler a toy and express interest in it, then offer the toy to the toddler—but tell the friend to "accidentally" drop the toy in such a way that the child can't access it (for example, behind a barrier). The other friend should also show the toddler a toy and express interest in it, but after offering the toy to the toddler, have her smile, say "Never mind," and put the toy away. Finally, put a new toy in front of your toddler and have both friends put their hands out and request it.

THE HYPOTHESIS

Your toddler is more likely to assist the friend who was willing but unable to give her the toy, as opposed to the friend who was able but not willing to give her the toy.

THE RESEARCH

In a 2010 experiment, 24 toddlers, all about 21 months old, stood behind a table with their parents behind them. Two women (hired actresses) stood on the other end of the table and offered the children a toy—but one withdrew the toy, while the other dropped it and acted as if it were lost. When the children were then given a toy, and both women reached for it, two-thirds of the children handed the toy to the woman who had unsuccessfully tried to give them a toy; the other eight kept the toy for themselves. Not a single child gave the toy to the woman who had offered a toy and then retracted the offer.

The experiment suggests that children, even at the earliest stages of helping behavior, are selective in how they choose to help; that reciprocation (helping those who have previously helped you) is at play in this selective behavior; and that toddlers take into account the intent of an attempted helpful action, even if the attempt is unsuccessful.

Indeed, a related experiment suggests that toddlers ascribe the same weight to an unsuccessful attempt at help as to a successful attempt. In this experiment, one woman tried unsuccessfully to give the child a toy, and the other successfully gave the child a toy. Then the child was given a toy, and both women requested it. The researchers noted that 16 out of 21 toddlers gave the toy to one of the women, and of those, half gave it to the woman who unsuccessfully tried to help, and the other half gave it to the one who successfully helped—suggesting that what matters more when children consider helping behavior is the intent, rather than the results.

 **THE TAKEAWAY**

Even at your baby's young age, she's not indiscriminate about whom she helps. Her decision may not be tactical (that is, helping the person who's more likely to come to her aid in the future) but it is definitely intentional: She rewards those who have helped her over those who haven't. Because this aspect of her social development helps her distinguish friends from adversaries, encourage older siblings to find ways to help her reach her goals, such as by helping her obtain a toy that's out of reach. It's a great way to strengthen the bond between them.

Punishing the Bad Guy

Age range: 19–23 months
Experiment complexity: Complex
Research area: Social development and emotional development

THE EXPERIMENT

Gather or construct three distinct-looking hand puppets. You'll also need a small ball and a handful of Cheerios or other similar cereal.

Introduce your child to the three puppets and ask him to feed some Cheerios to each puppet. The puppet should nibble on the Cheerios and respond as if the cereal was very tasty. Next, tell him that you're going to perform a puppet show. Act out the following scene: One puppet plays with a ball. The puppet drops the ball. Another puppet comes by, picks up the ball, and gives it back to the first puppet. The puppet drops the ball again. The third puppet comes by, picks up the ball, and runs away with it.

Finally, show your child the helper puppet (who returned the ball to its owner) and the hinderer puppet (who ran away with the ball). Say that there's only one Cheerio left, and allow him to choose which of the two puppets to give it to.

 ## THE HYPOTHESIS

Your baby is extremely likely to give the final Cheerio to the helper puppet, rather than the hinderer puppet.

 ## THE RESEARCH

In a 2011 study involving toddlers between 19 and 23 months, the researchers acted out a short puppet show with these scenarios. The toddlers were then given the opportunity to reward either the helper or hinderer with a piece of food. They overwhelmingly chose to reward the helper. Moreover, when they were given the chance to take away a piece of food from either the helper or the hinderer, they overwhelmingly chose to take the food away from the hinderer.

The results of this study show that by around the end of the first year, babies have moral intuitions that closely mirror those of adults: They prefer to reward those who display positive social behavior and punish those who display negative social behavior.

# THE TAKEAWAY

The results of this study suggest that even before their first birthday, babies have a rudimentary sense of right and wrong. Granted, they won't always act like they *care* about right and wrong, but at least they are able to recognize it when they see it. An opportune moment to help your child better understand the moral principles that underpin an action is when you are praising him for good behavior or correcting him for bad behavior. For instance, if he has shared a toy, you might point out that sharing is good because it shows others that you care for them and want them to be happy. Conversely, if he has thrown a toy, you might point out that throwing toys is wrong because it could hurt someone and because it does not show that he appreciates what he has.

Don't You Know?

Age range: 24 months

Experiment complexity: Moderate

Research area: Social development and cognitive development

THE EXPERIMENT

Gather three objects, each distinct in appearance, that are unfamiliar to your toddler but safe to play with (such as an empty wallet, a water bottle, or a ball of yarn). Have a friend join you and your toddler at a table. Present the first object, and have your friend express interest in it, using phrases like, "Look at that!" and "Isn't that neat?" Allow your toddler to play with the object for about 30 seconds. Then put away the first object and present the second object. Your friend should again express interest in it, and you should again let your toddler play with it for about 30 seconds. Now, put away the second object. At this point, your friend should turn his chair so he's facing away from the

table and unable to see it. Now, present the third object. Your friend should remain silent and should not turn around or look at the object. Let your toddler play with the third object for about 30 seconds, then put it away. After a brief pause, place all three objects on the table. At this point, your friend should turn his chair back around and say, without looking directly at any of the toys, "Wow, look! I don't know that one yet. Can you give it to me, please?" Make note of which object your toddler gives him.

THE HYPOTHESIS

The third object is the only one of the three that your friend did not see. But your toddler is unlikely to be able to identify it as the object that your friend doesn't know yet.

THE RESEARCH

In a 2010 study, 24-month-olds were shown three objects in succession. With the first two objects, an experimenter sat nearby and expressed interest in the objects. Before the third object was presented, some of the toddlers saw the experimenter get up and leave the room. Others saw a divider placed near the experimenter, blocking her ability to view the object. She nevertheless expressed interest in the object, despite not being able to see it. In the group in which the experimenter left the room, nearly two-thirds correctly identified the third object as the one the experimenter was referring to when she said, "I don't know that one yet." In contrast, in the group in which the experimenter remained nearby, fewer than one-third (less than chance) gave the third object to the experimenter.

The researchers say the results of this study show that when young children are socially engaged with a person and the person remains in proximity, they tend to operate as if that person occupies the same "perceptual space." In other words, they assume that if they can perceive an object, the other person can also perceive it.

The social engagement aspect of the experiment appears to be key to this illusion of occupying the same perceptual space because an earlier experiment showed that babies as young as 12 months old are able to realize that an adult sitting across from them cannot necessarily see the same things as them.

 **THE TAKEAWAY**

By age 2, your toddler is able to do all sorts of things. The number of words he can understand is vast, he is able to follow simple requests, and he's well on his way to being able to take off all his own clothes and go streaking. But the results of this experiment show that he's still prone to certain perceptual misunderstandings, particularly when he is socially engaged with someone. In a way, though, you should feel flattered: Your interaction with your child is so interesting to him that it leads him to overlook or misunderstand things he otherwise wouldn't. Your toddler will get better at this over time, without much need for active coaching, but in the meantime, be aware that your child may not be able to make perceptual space determinations with accuracy.

Don't Try This at Home

There are a few famous infant experiments that are really cool, but not DIY-friendly. One such experiment is called the Visual Cliff, which is intended to test depth perception. The apparatus used during the experiment is a raised platform with a patterned (often checkerboard) surface. In the middle of the platform, there is a clear plexiglass "bridge" that crosses over a "valley" with the same pattern as that on the platform. Babies are placed on the platform and prompted to crawl over the bridge. Research since the 1960s has shown that newly crawling infants tend to cross the Visual Cliff without hesitation, but those who have some crawling—and falling—experience tend to hesitate or refuse, which suggests that they have perceived the vertical drop-off and fear falling into it. Of course, the clear plexiglass will prevent them from falling, but that's not plainly obvious to the babies, so they stay away from the ledge.

Projects by Complexity

SIMPLE

1. Soothing Scents
2. Baby Blueprints
3. En Garde
4. Happy Feet
7. Response Under Pressure
8. I'm Hip to That
9. This Little Piggy Was Named Babinski
13. Tongue Testing
16. Spider Sense
21. Body Stretches
24. The Gestation of Gestures
25. Sizing Things Up
26. Mirror, Mirror
28. Grabby Hands
29. I Want What You Want
31. The In-Plain-Sight Switcheroo
33. The Importance of an Audience
34. A Gazy Connection
37. Defending What's Mine
41. The Retriever

MODERATE

5. A Penchant for Patterns
6. Feet Lead the Way
10. A Memorable Smile
11. Out on a Limb
12. Grasping Prep
14. Picture: Impossible
15. Pitch Patterns
18. The Face Matches the Feeling
19. Stress Busting
22. A Cappella Strikes a Chord
23. Natural Interference
27. Capturing the Cup
30. Be Still, My Face
35. Shapes or Kinds?
36. Demonstration and Deduction
38. Taking Cues
39. Walking Tour
40. Familiarity and Foods
42. I Know Something You Don't Know
43. Using Your Head

MODERATE (CONTINUED)

44. A Questioning Look
46. Same or Similar?
47. The Ambiguous "One"
48. Helping the Helper
50. Don't You Know?

COMPLEX

17. Put an Age to That Face
20. Propulsive Perceptions
32. The Goldilocks Effect
45. Power Napping
49. Punishing the Bad Guy

Projects by Research Area

References

1 SOOTHING SCENTS

Nishitani, Shota; Miyamura, Tsunetake; Tagawa, Masato; et al. The calming effect of a maternal breast milk odor on the human newborn infant. *Neuroscience Research* 63(1):66–71, January 2009.

Rattaz, Cécile; Goubet, Nathalie; and Bullinger, André. The calming effect of a familiar odor on full-term newborns. *Journal of Developmental & Behavioral Pediatrics* 26(2):86–92, April 2005.

2. BABY BLUEPRINTS

Macchi Cassia, Viola; Valenza, Eloisa; Simion, Francesca; and Leo, Irene. Congruency as a nonspecific perceptual property contributing to newborns' face preference. *Child Development* 79(4):807–820, July/August 2008.

Simion, Francesca; Valenza, Eloisa; Macchi Cassia, Viola; et al. Newborns' preference for up-down asymmetrical configurations. *Developmental Science* 5(4):427–434, November 2002.

3. EN GARDE

Haywood, Kathleen and Getchell, Nancy. *Life Span Motor Development* (5th ed.). Champaign, IL: Human Kinetics, 2009.

Pieper, Albrecht. *Cerebral Function in Infancy and Childhood.* New York: Consultants Bureau, 1963.

4. HAPPY FEET

Thelen, Esther; Fisher, Donna M.; and Ridley-Johnson, Robyn. The relationship between physical growth and a newborn reflex. *Infant Behavior and Development* 7(4):479–493, October–December 1984.

Thelen, Esther; Smith, Linda B.; Damon, William (ed.); and Lerner, Richard M. (ed.). Dynamic systems theories. *Handbook of Child Psychology* 1(5): 563–634. Hoboken, NJ: Wiley, 1998.

5. A PENCHANT FOR PATTERNS

Fantz, Robert L. Pattern vision in newborn infants. *Science* 140(3564): 296–297, April 19, 1963.

6. FEET LEAD THE WAY

Galloway, James C. and Thelen, Esther. Feet first: object exploration in young infants. *Infant Behavioral Development* 27(1):107–112, February 2004.

7. RESPONSE UNDER PRESSURE

Babkin, P. S. The establishment of reflex activity in early postnatal life. *The Central Nervous System and Behavior* (translated by the U.S. Department of Health, Education and Welfare). Washington, DC: Public Health Service, 1960.

Pedroso, Fleming S. and Rotta, Newra T. Babkin reflex and other motor responses to appendicular compression stimulus of the newborn. *Journal of Child Neurology* 19(8):592–596, August 2004.

8. I'M HIP TO THAT

Berne, Samuel A. The primitive reflexes: considerations in the infant. *Optometry & Vision Development* 37(3):139, September 2006.

9. THIS LITTLE PIGGY WAS NAMED BABINSKI

Singerman, Jennifer and Lee, Liesly. Consistency of the Babinski reflex and its variants. *European Journal of Neurology* 15(9):960–964, September 2008.

10. A MEMORABLE SMILE

Turati, Chiara; Montirosso, Rosario; Brenna, Viola; et al. A Smile enhances 3-month-olds' recognition of an individual face. *International Society on Infant Studies* 16(3):306–317, May–June 2011.

11. OUT ON A LIMB

Skinner, B. F. *The Behavior of Organisms: An Experimental Analysis.* New York: Appleton-Century-Crofts, 1938.

Watanabe, Hama and Taga, Gentaro. General to specific development of movement patterns and memory for contingency between actions and events in young infants. *Infant Behavior and Development* 29(3):402–422, September 2006.

12. GRASPING PREP

Bhat, Anjana N. and Galloway, James C. Toy-oriented changes during early arm movements: hand kinematics. *Infant Behavior & Development* 29(3): 358–372, July 2006.

13. TONGUE TESTING

Chen, Xin; Reid, Vincent M.; and Striano, Tricia. Oral exploration and reaching toward social and non-social objects in two-, four-, and six-month-old infants. *European Journal of Developmental Psychology* 3(1): 1–12, 2006.

14. PICTURE: IMPOSSIBLE

Shuwairi, Sarah M.; Albert, Marc K.; and Johnson, Scott P. Discrimination of possible and impossible objects in infancy. *Psychological Science* 18(4): 303–307, April 2007.

Shuwairi, Sarah M.; Tran, Annie; DeLoache, Judy S.; and Johnson, Scott P. Infants' responses to pictures of impossible objects. *Infancy* 15(6): 636–649, December 2010.

15. PITCH PATTERNS

Fox, Donna Brink. An analysis of the pitch characteristics of infant vocalizations. *Psychomusicology* 9(1):21–30, 1990.

Moog, Helmut. The development of musical experience in children of preschool age. *Psychology of Music* 4(2):38–45, 1976.

16. SPIDER SENSE

Rakison, David H. and Derringer, Jaime. Do infants possess an evolved spider-detection mechanism? *Cognition* 107(1):381–393, September 2007.

17. PUT AN AGE TO THAT FACE

Bahrick, Lorraine E.; Netto, Dianelys; and Hernandez-Reif, Maria. Intermodal perception of adult and child faces and voices by infants. *Child Development* 69(5):1263–1275, October 1998.

Greenberg, David J.; Hillman, Donald; and Grice, Dean. Infant and stranger variables related to stranger anxiety in the first year of life. *Developmental Psychology* 9(2):207–212, September 1973.

Walker-Andrews, Arlene S.; Bahrick, L. E.; Raglioni, S. S.; and Diaz, I. Infants' bimodal perception of gender. *Ecological Psychology* 3(2):55–75, 1991.

18. THE FACE MATCHES THE FEELING

Bennett, David S.; Bendersky, Margaret; and Lewis, Michael. Does the organization of emotional expression change over time? Facial expressivity from 4 to 12 months. *Infancy* 8(2):167–187, September 2005.

19. STRESS BUSTING

Crockenberg, Susan C. and Leerkes, Esther M. Infant and maternal behaviors regulate infant reactivity to novelty at 6 months. *Developmental Psychology* 40(6):1123–1132, November 2004.

Diener, M. L. and Mangelsdorf, S. C. Behavioral strategies for emotion regulation in toddlers: associations with maternal involvement and emotional expressions. *Infant Behavior & Development* 22(4):569–583, 1999.

Stifter, C. A. and Braungart, J. M. The regulation of negative reactivity in infancy: function and development. *Developmental Psychology* 31(3): 448–455, May 1995.

20. PROPULSIVE PERCEPTIONS

Cicchino, Jessica B. and Rakison, David H. Producing and processing self-propelled motion in infancy. *Developmental Psychology* 44(5):1232–1241, September 2008.

Markson, Lori and Spelke, Elizabeth S. Infants' rapid learning about self-propelled objects. *Infancy* 9(1):45–71, January 2006.

21. BODY STRETCHES

Slaughter, Virginia and Heron, Michelle. Origins and early development of human body knowledge. *Monographs of the Society for Research in Child Development* 69(2):1–113, 2004.

Zieber, Nicole; Bhatt, Ramesh S.; Hayden, Angela; et al. Body representation in the first year of life. *Infancy* 15(5):534–544, September–October 2010.

22. A CAPPELLA STRIKES A CHORD

Ilari, Beatriz and Polka, Linda. Music cognition in early infancy: infants' preferences and long-term memory for Ravel. *International Journal of Music Education* 24(1):7–20, April 2006.

Ilari, Beatriz and Sundara, Megha. Music listening preferences in early life. *Journal of Research in Music Education* 56(4):357–369, January 2009.

23. NATURAL INTERFERENCE

Newman, Rochelle S. The cocktail party effect in infants revisited: listening to one's name in noise. *Developmental Psychology* 41(2):352–362, March 2005.

Polka, Linda; Rvachew, Susan; and Molnar, Monika. Speech perception by 6- to 8-month-olds in the presence of distracting sounds. *Infancy* 13(5): 421–439, September 2008.

24. THE GESTATION OF GESTURES

Iverson, Jana M. and Fagan, Mary K. Infant vocal-motor coordination: precursor to the gesture-speech system? *Child Development* 75(4):1053–1066, July–August 2004.

Iverson, Jana M. and Thelen, Esther. Hand, mouth, and brain: the dynamic emergence of speech and gesture. *Journal of Consciousness Studies* 6(11–12):19–40, 1999.

25. SIZING THINGS UP

Corbetta, Daniela and Snapp-Childs, Winona. Seeing and touching: the role of sensory-motor experience on the development of infant reaching. *Infant Behavior and Development* 32(1):44–58, January 2009.

26. MIRROR, MIRROR

Fiamenghi, Geraldo A. Emotional expression in infants' interactions with their mirror images: an exploratory study. *Journal of Reproductive and Infant Psychology* 25(2):152–160, May 2007.

Amsterdam, Beulah. Mirror self-image reactions before age two. *Developmental Psychobiology* 5(4):297–305, 1972.

27. CAPTURING THE CUP

Daum, Moritz M.; Vuori, Maria T.; Prinz, Wolfgang; and Aschersleben, Gisa. Inferring the size of a goal object from an actor's grasping movement in 6- and 9-month-old infants. *Developmental Science* 12(6):854–862, November 2009.

von Hofsten, Claes and Ronnqvist, Louise. Preparation for grasping an object: a developmental study. *Journal of Experimental Psychology: Human Perception and Performance* 14(4):610–621, November 1988.

28. GRABBY HANDS

Fagard, Jacqueline and Marks, Anne. Unimanual and bimanual tasks and the assessment of handedness in toddlers. *Developmental Science* 3(2): 137–147, May 2000.

Fagard, Jacqueline; Spelke, Elizabeth; and von Hofsten, Claes. Reaching and grasping a moving object in 6-, 8-, and 10-month-old infants: laterality and performance. *Infant Behavior and Development* 32(2):137–146, 2009.

29. I WANT WHAT YOU WANT

Hamlin, J. Kiley; Hallinan, Elizabeth V.; and Woodward, Amanda L. Do as I do: 7-month-old infants selectively reproduce others' goals. *Developmental Science* 11(4):487–494, August 2008.

30. BE STILL, MY FACE

Meadow-Orlans, Kathryn P.; Spencer, Patricia Elizabeth; and Koester, Lynne Sanford. *The World of Deaf Infants: A Longitudinal Study*. New York: Oxford University Press, 2004.

Nadel, Jacqueline; Croue, Sabine; Mattlinger, Marie-Jeanne; et al. Do children with autism have expectations about the behaviours of unfamiliar people? *Autism* 4(2):133–145, June 2000.

31. THE IN-PLAIN-SIGHT SWITCHEROO

Munakata, Yuko. Perseverative reaching in infancy: the roles of hidden toys and motor history in the AB task. *Infant Behavior and Development* 20(3):405–416, July 1997.

Smith, Linda B.; Thelen, Esther; Titzer, Robert; and McLin, Dewey. Knowing in the context of acting: the task dynamics of the A-not-B error. *Psychological Review* 106(2):235–260, April 1999.

32. THE GOLDILOCKS EFFECT

Kidd, Celeste; Piantadosi, Steven T.; and Aslin, Richard N. The Goldilocks effect: human infants allocate attention to visual sequences that are neither too simple nor too complex. *PLoS ONE* 7(5):e36399, May 2012.

33. THE IMPORTANCE OF AN AUDIENCE

Goldstein, Michael H.; King, Andrew P.; and West, Meredith J. Social interaction shapes babbling: testing parallels between birdsong and speech. *Proceedings of the National Academy of the Sciences of the United States of America* 100(13):8030–8035, 2003.

34. A GAZY CONNECTION

Beier, Jonathan S. and Spelke, Elizabeth S. Infants' developing understanding of social gaze. *Child Development* 83(2):486–496, March–April 2012.

35. SHAPES OR KINDS?

Dewar, Kathryn and Xu, Fei. Do early nouns refer to kinds or distinct shapes? Evidence from 10-month-old infants. *Psychological Science* 20(2):252–257, February 2009.

36. DEMONSTRATION AND DEDUCTION

Elsner, Birgit; Hauf, Petra; and Aschersleben, Gisa. Imitating step by step: a detailed analysis of 9- to 15-month-olds' reproduction of a three-step action sequence. *Infant Behavior & Development* 30(2):325–335, May 2007.

37. DEFENDING WHAT'S MINE

Hay, Dale; Hurst, Sarah-Louise; Waters, Cerith; and Chadwick, Andrea. Infants' use of force to defend toys: the origins of instrumental aggression. *Infancy* 16(5):471–489, September/October 2011.

38. TAKING CUES

Corkum, Valerie and Moore, Chris. The origin of joint visual attention in infants. *Developmental Psychology* 34(1):28–38, January 1998.

Mumme, Donna L. and Fernald, Anne. The infant as onlooker: learning from emotional reactions observed in a television scenario. *Child Development* 74(1):221–237, February 2003.

39. WALKING TOUR

Adolph, Karen E.; Vereijken, Beatrix; and Shrout, Patrick E. What changes in infant walking and why. *Child Development* 74(2):475–497, March 2003.

40. FAMILIARITY AND FOODS

Shutts, Kristin; Kinzler, Katherine D.; McKee, Caitlin B.; and Spelke, Elizabeth S. Social information guides infants' selection of foods. *Journal of Cognitive Development* 10(1–2):1–17, January 2009.

41. THE RETRIEVER

Karasik, Lana B.; Tamis-LeMonda, Catherine S.; and Adolph, Karen E. Transition from crawling to walking and infants' actions with objects and people. *Child Development* 82(4):1199–1209, July–August 2011.

42. I KNOW SOMETHING YOU DON'T KNOW

Baron-Cohen, Simon. The development of a theory of mind in autism: deviance and delay. *The Psychiatric Clinics of North America* 14(1):33–51, March 1991.

Onishi, Kristine H. and Baillargeon, Renée. Do 15-month-old infants understand false beliefs? *Science* 308(5719):255–258, April 8, 2005.

Surian, Luca; Caldi, Stefania; and Sperber, Dan. Attribution of beliefs by 13-month-old infants. *Psychological Science* 18(7):580–586, July 2007.

43. USING YOUR HEAD

Gergely, György; Bekkering, Harold; and Király, Ildikó. Rational imitation in preverbal infants. *Nature* 415(6873):755, February 14, 2002.

Paulus, Markus; Hunnius, Sabine; Vissers, Marlies; and Bekkering, Harold. Imitation in infancy: rational or motor resonance? *Child Development* 82(4):1047–1057, July–August 2011.

44. A QUESTIONING LOOK

Vaish, Amrisha; Demir, Özlem Ece; and Baldwin, Dare. Thirteen- and 18-month-old infants recognize when they need referential information. *Social Development* 20(3):431–449, August 2011.

45. POWER NAPPING

Gomez, Rebecca L.; Bootzin, Richard R.; and Nadel, Lynn. Naps promote abstraction in language-learning infants. *Psychological Science* 17(8):670–674, August 2006.

Mander, Bryce A.; Santhanam, Sangeetha; Saletin, Jared M.; and Walker, Matthew P. Wake deterioration and sleep restoration of human learning. *Current Biology* 21(5):183–184, March 8, 2011.

46. SAME OR SIMILAR?

Stager, C. L. and Werker, J. F. Infants listen for more phonetic detail in speech perception than in word-learning tasks. *Nature* 388(6640):381–382, July 24, 1997.

Werker, Janet F.; Fennell, Christopher T.; Corcoran, Kathleen M.; and Stager, Christine L. Infants' ability to learn phonetically similar words: effects of age and vocabulary size. *Infancy* 3(1):1–30, January 2002.

47. THE AMBIGUOUS "ONE"

Lidz, Jeffrey; Waxman, Sandra; and Freedman, Jennifer. What infants know about syntax but couldn't have learned: experimental evidence for syntactic structure at 18 months. *Cognition* 89(3):65–73, October 2003.

48. HELPING THE HELPER

Dunfield, Kristen A. and Kuhlmeier, Valerie A. Intention-mediated selective helping in infancy. *Psychological Science* 21(4):523–527, April 2010.

49. PUNISHING THE BAD GUY

Hamlin, J. Kiley; Wynn, Karen; Bloom, Paul; and Mahajan, Neha. How infants and toddlers react to antisocial others. *Proceedings of the National Academy of Sciences of the United States of America* 108:19931–19936, 2011.

50. DON'T YOU KNOW?

Moll, Henrike; Carpenter, Malinda; and Tomasello, Michael. Social engagement leads 2-year-olds to overestimate others' knowledge. *Infancy* 16(3): 248–265, May/June 2010.

Luo, Yuyan; and Baillargeon, Renée. Do 12.5-month-old infants consider what objects others can see when interpreting their actions? *Cognition* 105(3):489–512, December 2007.

DON'T TRY THIS AT HOME

Page 40: Dyer, Jim. Ethics and orphans: the "monster study." *San Jose Mercury News*, June 10, 2001.

Page 135: Bain, Katherine; Faegre, Marion L.; and Wyly, Robert S. Behavior of young children under conditions simulating entrapment in refrigerators. *Pediatrics* 22(4):628–647, October 1958.

Acknowledgments

Joel and Ben, my sweet sons, who inspired me to write this book, and who inspire me in many other ways.

Tanya, my beautiful wife, who gave me the OK to introduce even more craziness into our already crazy lives.

Betty and Frank, my parents, who made many sacrifices so that I could have more opportunities than they did.

Marina Koren, my research assistant, who went above and beyond.

Maria Gagliano, who guided the book through its early stages.

Marian Lizzi, my editor, whose insight and attention to detail have been invaluable.

Laurie Abkemeier, my agent, who has patiently guided me through the publishing process and given me so much spot-on advice.

Adam Ruben and Marina Koestler Ruben, fellow authors who shared their own experiences and gave me some hot tips.

Daniel Herd and Amy Conver, who helped road test several experiments.

The Perigee staff, true collaborators.

About the Author

Shaun Gallagher, a father of two ongoing science experiments, is a writer and former magazine and newspaper editor. He also runs the popular website Correlated.org, which analyzes statistical data to find funny and surprising correlations. He lives in Wilmington, Delaware. Visit ExperimentingWithBabies.com for baby research news, additional experiments, and interactive features for new parents.